EDUCATION OF A WANDERING YOUNG MAN

C S LAM

PARTRIDGE

To order additional copies of this book, contact
Toll Free +65 3165 7531 (Singapore)
Toll Free +60 3 3099 4412 (Malaysia)
orders.singapore@partridgepublishing.com

To contact the author for talks and other matters, write to
cslam0166@gmail.com

www.partridgepublishing.com/singapore

CONTENTS

DEDICATION

To the family God has blessed me with: my wife, Sandra, and my three children, Reuben, Ruth and Raphael.

To my spiritual parents and friends in Loughborough, who encouraged me to grow in God.

To all my students – past, present and future – who desire to live life to the fullest.

ACKNOWLEDGEMENTS

I owe the completion of this book to the following:

*   My wife, Sandra, for reading through my draft and giving me invaluable input to polish my language and make the content more comprehensible for the reader.

*   My friends in Hakka Methodist Church who prayed for strength and perseverance for me to complete this writing project.

*   My former teachers and professors who taught me to read and write, and to enjoy poetry.

*   Public Service Commission (PSC) for granting me the scholarship to the United Kingdom, without which I would not have the means to travel widely.

*   God for giving me the ability and stamina to write despite my poor sleep in the past year.

INTRODUCTION

This book came 25 years late. Still, I am thankful that it came. If not for the 'circuit breaker lockdown' in Singapore from 7 April to 1 June 2020, which was introduced by the government to curb the spread of Covid-19, this book might never have seen the light of day.

I have always wanted to write a book about my travels. A few years before I turned thirty, my sister bought me a T-shirt as a birthday present. The words that were printed on it, 'I wrote my first book before I turn thirty', became my secret wish. However, as was the case for most young people in Singapore, the natural events of life just consumed all my time and energy. From full time teaching to marriage to starting a family, and moving house three times in the space of three and a half years after my marriage, there was no time to sit down, recollect and reflect on my wandering days. Then Covid-19 came into this world and imposed a lockdown in many countries in 2020, including Singapore. A summer course that I was supposed to teach from late April to early August 2020 was cancelled as the foreign participants were not allowed to enter Singapore. All of a sudden, I was blessed with much time.

This book was birthed by the Covid-19 pandemic. With no teaching duties, I started writing this book on 5th May 2020 during the Covid-19 circuit breaker lockdown. By the end of July, in mere three months, I had finished writing eight chapters, up to my eleven-week East African journey. In those three months, I was also reading *Wild Swans*, a thick novel which won the 1992 NCR Book Award, a second time, so as to conduct a strictly voluntary class through Zoom for six PRC Chinese scholars who were studying in Nanayang Technological University (NTU). Due to the pandemic, none of them could go home that summer, and it was my aim to occupy them with a novel which they possibly had no legal access to in China. As it turned out, the reading of *Wild Swans* helped me scrutinize the descriptive and narrative writing style of Jung Chang, the well-known writer, and to learn from her.

Apart from my writing style, I was also mindful about the accuracy of every detail I included in my writing. To help me write about events which happened more than thirty years ago with accuracy and authenticity, I relied on multiple sources: my travel diaries, photographs and slides, letters and postcards sent (some of them) and received, physical maps, bus and train tickets, and of course research on the internet. When none of the above sources could ascertain the events I was writing about, I turned to my imagination and human logic to fill in the gaps. Thus, I could confidently claim that the accounts narrated in this book are more than 95 percent factual and accurate.

This book is essentially about my travels to different countries from December 1986 to December 1991. In those five years, I had the privilege to set foot on five continents, and interacted with people of diverse nationalities and ethnic tribes. The experiences had enriched my life beyond the confines of the four walls of a classroom; they constituted a form of education which I consider superior to the conventional approach through books and the internet. This explains why the first word of the title of this book is 'Education'. Invariably, after visiting each country, I had a better understanding and appreciation of the history and culture of that land, and to some extent, also the social and political issues faced by the general population. Education acquired through this means is not likely to be forgotten even after an examination; on the contrary, it is likely to remain with one forever.

It is my sincere hope that readers the world over will find my travel experiences interesting. When the world is fully open after the pandemic, may they be inspired to go on physical journeys to explore exotic lands and be educated by the world.

PERSONAL PHOTOGRAPHS
AND SKETCHES

Christmas 1986 with Dirk and his
mother at Montabaur, Germany

Day outing to Caesarea with volunteers
from Nirim Kibbutz, Israel

With Mohamed at Quarzazate, Morocco

Five high school girls who gave me a pen, Assisi, Italy

Members of Kalinda family, Zambia

With a Masai man at Masai Mara, Kenya

With my guide at Bario, East Malaysia

Happy faces at Karimabad, Pakistan

An Afghan family seeking refugee
status in New Delhi, India

With fellow Operation Raleigh
participants at Nireguao, Chile

Meal with Rosemary (left) and Guy Bookless
(foreground) and other international students

Bill and Joan Robertson, and Joanne
(middle), their youngest daughter

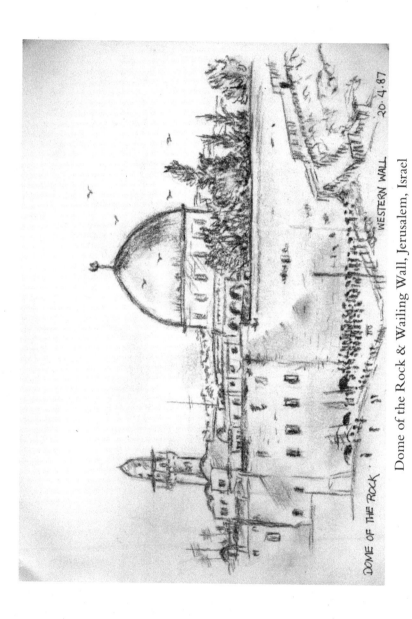

Dome of the Rock & Wailing Wall, Jerusalem, Israel

Kalinda Farm, Nega Nega, Zambia

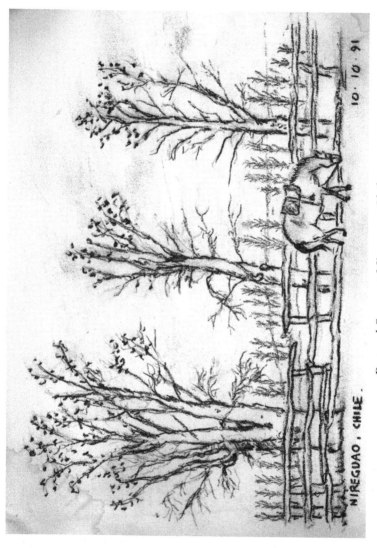

Pastoral Scene at Nireguao, Chile

Hanging Glacier, Queulat National Park, Chile

CHAPTER 1

Growing Awareness of a Larger World

"There is a time for everything, and a season for every activity under heaven."

Ecclesiastes 3:1

Growing up in post-independent Singapore in the seventies in a family of six members all squeezed into a one-room government flat, I lived in a cloistered world. My world consisted of my family, my neighbors who spoke a variety of Chinese dialects, even Malay and Tamil, and my school which was a stone's throw away. With no internet, no telephone at home, no access to newspapers and magazines, I had neither contact with, nor any concerns for, the world outside of my small neighborhood in Lengkok Bahru, near Redhill. All I was concerned about, apart from attending school, was to play football with some school friends and neighbors' children, watch television on our 16-inch black and white TV, and perform the household chores assigned to me. One of the tasks assigned to me was to lay the floor of the living-cum-bedroom with thick cardboards at night (so that we would not have to sleep on the cold cement floor) and to stash them away in the morning so that we would not step onto them and dirty them.

My first awareness of the existence of other countries came in my lower primary school days when my form teacher invited some of the students to join her philatelic club. The club gathered on some Saturday mornings during which the teacher would introduce us to some stamps of the world. I remembered her informing us that there is a country whose stamps do not need to display the name of its country because it is the first country to invent the use of postage stamps. In place of its name, the stamp bears the portrait of its ruling monarch; this country is the United Kingdom. At that time, I had absolutely no idea where this country was located, nor did I think it important to find out; it was to me a country far far away from Singapore. Soon after I started joining the philatelic club, I must have asked my father for some stamps because I recalled him periodically giving me a small packet of used stamps cut out from envelopes. These stamps came from China, the country my paternal and maternal grandparents came from. Little did I know then that these two countries, the United Kingdom and China, were to be my second and third home respectively in the ensuing years.

As I began my secondary school education, my horizons were widened through the study of Geography and History. In the former subject, I learnt about Australia and New Zealand in the first year and Europe and Africa in the second; in the latter subject, I was introduced to the ancient history of India, China, Babylon, Greece and Rome. I plunged myself deep into these two subjects, spending a disproportionate amount of time collecting brochures from some embassies and doing scrap books on some of these countries. There was no internet then and all forms of research had to be done through ploughing hard copies of books and magazines. Through it all, I learned about the names of many countries, their capital cities, their weather conditions, their main agricultural produce, and at times even forms of government. However, despite my interest in these countries, I found it difficult to remember certain facts. In one of the Geography tests, I could not remember if winter occurs in Dec-Feb or Jun-Aug in Australia, and I picked the wrong answer. It was then that I told myself that the best way to learn is not to memorize facts but to experience life in other countries. If I had an opportunity to live in a country with four seasons, I would not have any difficulty answering a question about when winter occurs in the southern hemisphere.

The presence of expatriate teachers in my secondary school (a rarity in those days) also gave me the exposure to the outside world. I had a Canadian teacher who taught my class Literature in my third year. We studied *The Grapes of Wrath* by John Steinbeck (an extremely difficult book for secondary three students, I must confess) and I was introduced to the effects of drought on farmers and names of states like Oklahoma and California in the United States. The following year, a Scottish teacher taught my class *Macbeth*, a Shakespeare's play. Not having had any prior exposure to the Scottish accent, we found it extremely difficult to understand him fully, though on hindsight it was a privilege few schools in Singapore had, to have a Scottish teacher teach a play about the ambitions of a Scottish general turned king. Nevertheless, the presence of this teacher exposed me to the real Scottish accent which I was to encounter years later in the United Kingdom.

In my junior college years, there were several talks on overseas scholarships conducted mostly by some government agencies. Typically, at such talks, students would hear about overseas studies in the United Kingdom, Australia and even New Zealand, and a few would be sent to the United States. Though I was not sure about procuring an overseas scholarship based on my academic results, I secretly wished that I could somehow be given one so that I could truly educate myself with regard to the world, not by rote learning but by experiencing life overseas. Deep within me, I yearned to visit some of the countries I had studied in lower secondary Geography classes, like the United Kingdom and Germany. In the latter country, I could also put my 'O' level German to good use. However, such a latent desire did not have the power to motivate me to focus more on my studies rather than my extra-curricular activities. I was fully engaged in my responsibilities as a scout leader, a rugby player and an athlete.

Soon after the 'A' level examinations, while waiting to be enlisted into National Service (NS), I found myself a temporary job at a construction site through a neighbor who lived in the same block of flats. For helping him carry equipment and make onsite measurements, I was paid a daily wage of $20, which was a reasonable sum in 1984. After working for some weeks, I had saved enough money to go on a four-day tour of West Malaysia, which I did together with three other scout leaders, all waiting for NS enlistment in March. Although it was not my first trip in

West Malaysia, that particular trip was special to me for a few reasons: it marked the beginning of my independent travels; it was fully self-funded; it signified my entry into adulthood. I gained confidence in planning my travels and executing the plans; I had grown wings that would allow me to 'fly' to wherever I desired to visit.

I was pleasantly surprised by my 'A' level results and went on to apply to read Law in National University of Singapore (NUS). A few months later, I was informed that a place had been reserved for me to begin my studies two years later, after the completion of my NS in 1987. This was good news but strangely it did not stir me to great heights of ecstasy. In the meantime, I was undergoing military training, from Basic Military Training (BMT) to Officer Cadet School (OCS) to Guards Officer Conversion Course (GOCC), and my ultimate goal was to complete it all as soon as possible. After what seemed like eternity, I was finally posted to 3rd Guards Battalion as a platoon commander. It was around this time that my elder sister came home one day with a Public Service Commission (PSC) overseas scholarship application form. Not thinking too much about it, I duly completed the form and submitted it to PSC. My focus then was on working harmoniously with my platoon sergeant, a regular soldier in the Singapore Armed Forces, and preparing the platoon for a major overseas training exercise in Brunei.

Not long after returning from the training in Brunei, I received news that I had been accepted to study a double degree in English & Physical Education and Sports Science in Loughborough University of Technology. I was overjoyed; I was going to the United Kingdom; I was going to be educated by the world. Having completed the training in OCS, I was commissioned as an officer; now,

I am given the title of a scholar; without doubt, I told myself I would become a gentleman, an erudite one that would be trained not just by the university but also by the world. These thoughts pervaded my mind, and thus in no time and with no uncertainty, I wrote to NUS to give up the opportunity to read Law the following year. To me, an overseas education with all the attendant exposure and opportunities was definitely a better form of education. It was with such a mindset that I prepared myself to leave Singapore for the United Kingdom in September 1986. To this day, I have no regrets.

Map 1: Belgium & Germany

CHAPTER 2

Going Solo to Germany

"You hem me in – behind and before; you have laid your hand upon me. Such knowledge is too wonderful for me, too lofty for me to attain."

Psalm 139: 5-6

With all the excitement that studying in a new country offered, I plunged myself fully into a new lifestyle of sports and books in Loughborough. At times, scenes of the Temburong jungle in Brunei still flashed across my mind, reminding me of the military life I had had not too long ago, and giving me a surreal feeling of my academic pursuit in an entirely new country and university. With a full timetable and countless assessments, the weeks went by very quickly, and daylight hours became shorter and shorter as winter approached. I remember leaving the classroom at 5 p.m. one day only to find that the sky had already darkened. However, my excitement grew as the first academic trimester of ten weeks drew to an end. Even as I was preparing for some end-of-term assessments, I was getting ready for my first solo trip to Germany!

I left Loughborough on a coach bound for London on the morning of 12 December 1986. The journey took about three hours. Once there, I met up with a few fellow scholars studying in London and Cambridge. Then, eight of us took a train to Dover where we boarded a ferry to cross the English Channel and arrived at Ostend, a coastal city in Belgium. We visited Bruges, a city known for its laces, canals, cobbled streets and medieval buildings, and Brussels, the capital city of Belgium. Apart from marveling at the old architecture in these cities, appreciating the large collection of art pieces in various museums, and being intrigued by the Manneken Pis, a 61-cm bronze sculpture of a naked boy urinating into a small fountain in the centre of Brussels, we enjoyed eating and chatting together. All in all, we spent four days in Belgium.

While it was enjoyable to have friends to travel with in Belgium, I was also glad to venture solo to Germany while the rest turned southward to France. Travelling in a group of eight had its own disadvantages; rather frequently, we had to spend time waiting for one another, and our choice of activities had to be curtailed in order to accommodate the choice of the majority. In addition, travelling in a group would not encourage one to break out of the comfort zone to meet and interact with fellow travelers from other countries and cultures, as one would feel obliged to spend time with one's travelling companions. For these reasons, and also due to an innate desire to travel solo, I was ready to bid the group farewell as I boarded a train to Aachen, the westernmost city of Germany, near the borders with Belgium and the Netherlands.

The first thing that struck me upon my arrival in Aachen was the familiarity of the language. I could read some of the words on signboards, billboards and posters. Armed with some German, I proceeded to the local tourist office to ask for a city map, my source of security in a new place. Given my shoestring budget, I could only spend the night at a youth hostel and use my money sparingly. At the local Christmas market, Weihnachtsmarkt, where crowds of people thronged, I immersed myself in the festive mood, convincing myself that I was a man alone not feeling the loneliness of this world. I took many photos for keepsake but refrained from spending too much on souvenirs and cards, beautiful as they were. However, I did invest in a pocket-sized English-German dictionary as I figured that it would be beneficial for me, not only to understand some German words that I would be coming across in the next few days, but also to improve my overall German vocabulary. On the way to the youth hostel, I bought two slices of beef from a meat shop which I cooked for myself in the hostel. While I enjoyed having communal meals with friends in Belgium, it was a refreshing change to eat all by myself this time.

Travelling by myself also allowed me to make friends easily, especially with fellow solo travelers. From them, I could often gather much useful information with regard to accommodation, mode of transport and practices that would enhance security and convenience for solo travelers. For instance, I learned from an American how to deposit my backpack in a locker at the Aachen railway station using a one-mark (German currency) coin. That would make walking about and frequenting museums in the city much faster and more convenient. As a result, I was able to visit two museums in Aachen in one morning, before boarding a train to Cologne in the early afternoon. The first was the Neue Galerie-Sammlung Ludwig Museum, which housed an internationally renowned collection of 20th century art; the second was Couven Musuem, with a collection of middle-class furnishings and decor from the 18th and early-19th centuries. I was delighted with my productivity and new-found freedom to move from one gallery to another as fast as I wished to, or to linger a little longer if some exhibits really interested me. For this reason, I was convinced of the benefits of traveling solo.

Such a conviction was severely challenged at the next stop in Cologne. Upon arrival at the railway station, I collected a city map and then bought myself some meat for dinner. However, as I found out, the old youth hostel had closed down and the new one was much further away from the city centre, and difficult to locate as it was already dark. In my quest to find the hostel, I had to cross a busy multi-lane highway. I stole a quick glance to my right and proceeded to cross it, totally oblivious to the fact that unlike Singapore and the United Kingdom, in continental Europe, I should be looking out for on-coming traffic from my left. As I was crossing the highway along the river Rhine, a vehicle whizzed past me, missing me by perhaps a few centimetres. I instantaneously halted, gripped by fear. Many questions flooded my mind: What if I had been injured or killed in Cologne? Who would come to my rescue? How would my family react to such news? I was visibly shaken by this close encounter with death in Cologne on a cold mid-December night! At the same time, it dawned upon me that a Higher Being had just saved me, that I was not travelling solo but with this Savior. Secretly, I asked this benevolent being to protect me for the rest of my trip.

The next morning, still recovering from the shock of near death and thankful to my Savior for saving me, I walked into a big church, Cologne Cathedral, to show my gratitude. The majestic columns within the cathedral and the vastness of it impressed upon me the pervasive presence of God. Whether I truly believed in the existence of God in my mind then was not a question; in my heart, I was overwhelmed with the intimate presence and touch of God. And I felt that I should spend some time exploring this huge cathedral wherein God's presence was palpable. So I paid an entrance fee of one mark to climb to the top of one of the towers. As I neared the top of the spiral stairs, little droplets of rainwater greeted me like water to a tired soul, and I was rewarded with a magnificent view of the entire city of Cologne. In my mind, I thought, 'This must be a semblance of how God sees His creation from heaven above.' I thanked God for such a divine revelation.

The rest of my time in Cologne was spent exploring museums. The Roman-Germanic Museum is an archaeological museum that houses a large collection of Roman artifacts from the Roman settlement when this city was part of the Roman Empire. I saw history come alive through the slabs of stones, statues, portraits, wall-paintings, mosaics and exquisite tableware used in Roman Cologne. Informative as this museum was to me, I found the Wallraf-Richartz Museum more appealing as it contained fine art from the 14th to early 20th century, housing important Gothic, Renaissance and Impressionist collections. At the museum bookshop, I was tempted to buy some postcards of the famous paintings in the museum but decided against that as my limited budget had to last me another week in Germany.

Despite my budget constraint, I visited a pub. I thought it meaningful for me to drink a glass of Kolsch beer, a style of beer originating from Cologne, while I was in this city. After a refreshing glass of beer, as I was about to leave the pub, the bartender offered me another glass of beer. This, I was told, was courtesy of another patron standing nearby. I was pleasantly surprised and thanked that man profusely in German, "Danke schön!" Needless to say, I picked up enough courage to converse with him in simple and broken German. This was my introduction to the German beer culture.

More surprises were to await me as I travelled south to Bonn. At the tourist office in Bonn, I was informed that the youth hostel in town was closed with effect from that day; instead, I was directed to take a bus which brought me straight to the doorstep of the youth hostel in Godesberg, some ten kilometres southeast of Bonn. In that hostel, I met a Belgian, an Israeli, a New Zealander couple and an Argentine. It was an unplanned gathering of many nationalities. Somehow, all of us struck a sweet accord with one another and began chatting and exchanging travel information like good old friends. We even took turns to introduce songs of our own mother tongues to the group, beginning with a song in Hebrew and moving on to Portuguese, Flemish, Chinese and English. It was truly a night of cultural exchange and great companionship. We had so much fun that we only retired to bed at one o'clock in the morning, but not before we took some photos and exchanged our addresses. Unknown to me then, I was to find myself travelling to the country of one of these companions in my next university vacation.

To be honest, I never felt lonely as I travelled by myself. In the youth hostel at Godesberg, I shared a dormitory with two others: a Belgian and an Israeli. Together with another lone traveler from Argentina, the four of us explored the sights and sounds of Bonn, such as visiting Beethoven's House, the 18th-century house where Beethoven was born; strolling in the botanical gardens of Poppelsdorf Castle, an 18th-century palace, and along River Rhine; and lingering over the Christmas market where we sipped cups of hot red wine. We provided companionship to one another but it was never obligatory; one could go a separate way if one so desired, as did the Belgian who left us after visiting Beethoven's House, and reunited with us at the youth hostel in the evening. We had an unspoken understanding that we were together for a brief period of time, but that did not stop us from sharing our joy with one another.

The next morning, the Israeli discovered snow on the ground and shared his joy with us immediately. We were all ecstatic, especially me as this was my first encounter with snow. At the Belgian's suggestion, the three of us walked up to Godesberg Castle and feasted on the beautiful white landscape around us. In a postcard featuring the River Rhine, I wrote from Godesberg to my sister and family back in Singapore: 'My trip is getting more exciting but also coming to an end in about 5 days' time. It is so white now, outside the window. Pure immaculate snow. Looks as though Christmas is going to be white... I love it and want all of you to share it.'

The white landscape mesmerized me as I travelled further south along River Rhine and River Moselle to a small town called Cochem. The slow train ride along River Moselle was especially scenic with hills on both sides of the river blanketed with snow, and once every so often, clusters of houses were seen huddling together along the riverbank, as though providing warmth to one another. I arrived in Cochem intoxicated by the breathtaking scenery around me. That evening, I was shocked to be told that I would be the only guest in the youth hostel; thank goodness, I had earlier bought a bottle of Mosel wine for DM 5 to keep me company for the night and to further intoxicate myself.

The next morning, I took a day trip to Trier, a city of extreme beauty and charm, according to several backpackers. Said to be the oldest city in Germany, Trier has many historical buildings to offer visitors, but unfortunately many were closed during winter and just before Christmas. However, I did enjoy roaming around the Christmas market and soaking in the festive cheer. Wanting to learn some German Christmas carols, I bought a Christmas cassette there, only to find out later that it contained just Christmas music with no songs. In life, one does not always get what one wants. Still I was thankful for the brief visit to Trier and to have bought a Christmas cassette for memory.

My last stop in Germany was Koblenz, located at the confluence of two rivers, Rhine and Moselle. Guided more by necessity rather than choice, I decided to spend Christmas in this city as the youth hostel here was one of the few that would remain open during Christmas. Situated on top of a hill overlooking the city of Koblenz, this youth hostel looked more like a castle to me from which one could see the "German Corner" (Deutsches Eck), a small strip of land at the confluence that houses a 37-metre high equestrian monument. I met two French girls in the hostel and learned for the first time of a railway strike. Due to such a strike, they were not able to make it back to Paris and had to spend Christmas eve in this hostel. While I was sure the strike had caused them great inconvenience, I was nevertheless glad that I was not going to be the only guest in this hostel.

Christmas in Koblenz was special and memorable. In the morning, Dirk, the hostel boy came to wake me up for breakfast. I was not sure why he did that but when I arrived at the dining room, the two French girls were already seated. After breakfast, the two girls asked me to join them in their walk into town which I gladly obliged. We descended some stairs and soon were walking along River Rhine and into a church, Basilica of Saint Castor, the oldest in Koblenz, featuring Romanesque architecture, just in time for the Christmas service. How much of the service or its significance I understood at that time I did not ask myself; all I knew was that it was Christmas day and therefore it was appropriate for me to attend a Christmas service, not forgetting that just a week ago, I had an epiphany of God saving me on a highway in Cologne.

After the service, we stopped by briefly at the "German Corner" and then decided to head straight back to the hostel due to the extreme cold and chill. By the time we had finished lunch, the snow had thickened to about two inches, and lured us outdoors to play with it. This we did but not for long, as the biting cold gnawed persistently at us, driving us indoors once again to sit in front of the television. Soon, a man appeared to fetch the two girls. We parted ways; I was glad to have had their company for half a day, and to have received four French kisses, two from each of them! In the evening, the warden of the youth hostel suggested that I follow Dirk to visit his parents at a youth hostel at Montabaur, northeast of Koblenz. I spent some time with his family, and before we left, Dirk's mother surprised me with a packet of chocolates—Christmas gift!

My experiences in Germany had been extraordinary: near death, hospitality from a stranger in a German pub, a spontaneous cultural night, snow, a Christmas service, four French kisses and a surprise Christmas gift. As I ventured from one place to another, I knew not what experiences would befall me but I had the tacit knowledge that all would be fine. I had learned so much about life from this solo trip; I had also grown in my awareness of a benevolent divine being travelling with me.

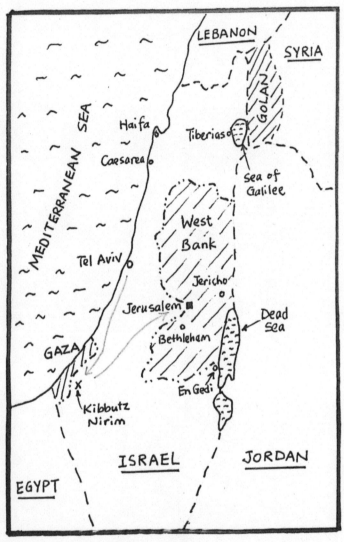

Map 2: Israel

CHAPTER 3

Learning Much in Israel

"Call to me and I will answer you and tell you great and unsearchable things you do not know."

Jeremiah 33:3

O nce back in Loughborough, I plunged straight back to my studies and sports. I had also started attending Elim Pentecostal Church on a regular basis. In one of the services in January 1987, I stepped forward to be prayed for when the preacher issued a call to the congregation to receive Christ so that "Christ could change you!" I remembered going forward for prayer not so much to receive Christ into my life but to test the claim by the preacher that Christ could change me. From the deepest core of my heart, I wanted to prove the preacher wrong.

It was my practice then to spend Sunday morning in church, relaxing or playing football with friends in the afternoon, and writing letters to family and friends in the evening. By mid-March, through letters, I had already confirmed with Ilan, the Israeli I met in Germany, that I would visit him in his country during my Easter vacation. I would work as a volunteer in his kibbutz, a collective agricultural community in Israel, for three weeks and travel round the country the rest of the time. In this way, I would be entitled to free food and lodging while working in the kibbutz, leaving me with enough money to spend for the last eleven days. Born and raised in a city state, I did not have any prior knowledge of farm life and thus was looking forward to my time in the kibbutz.

The weeks leading up to my departure to Israel, there was much news about bombing and shelling in some parts of Israel. Naturally, such news could cause one intending to visit the country some disturbance and unease. However, a few days before I left for Israel, Selvam, my best friend and a fellow Singaporean studying in the same university, came to share his dream with me. In his dream, he saw a sheep straying from the flock and the shepherd gently guiding the strayed sheep home. Selvam told me I was the sheep and God, the shepherd who would be guiding me as I went on this journey to Israel. His interpretation of the dream was comforting to me; internally, I wanted to believe in God's watchful eyes over me as I embarked on this trip to Israel.

The plane touched down at Ben Gurion Airport in Tel Aviv at 4 a.m. on 26 March 1987. My first impression was one of finally being home: the palm trees and the familiar morning chill reminded me of Singapore, or some places in Southeast Asia; the surrounding distinctly informed me that I had left Europe. Following some instructions given to me, I took a bus from the airport to Tel Aviv central bus station. At one of the many stops, a soldier with a rifle slung across his arm came up, glanced hastily at the passengers and then went down. It was a normal routine check for suspicious characters, but it indicated the high level of alertness the country was in. At Tel Aviv central bus station, I saw more young people in army uniform, male and female, all with a rifle slung over their arms. It finally sank in: I had arrived in a country that is ready for war.

Another bus ride heading south towards Gaza Strip and lasting more than one and a half hours brought me nearer to my final destination: Kibbutz Nirim. Early kibbutzim were often strategically located along the country's borders and outlying areas in order to help in the defense of the country. Founded in 1946, Kibbutz Nirim is situated some two kilometres west from the border of Gaza Strip, and surrounded by vast stretches of farmland. In the kibbutz, I was assigned a simple room with a bed, a table and a chair in the volunteers' quarters. Among the foreign volunteers in the kibbutz then were two French ladies, one Austrian lady, an Irish, two Brazilians, one Uruguayan, three Mexican ladies, two Australians, a Japanese, an English and an Israeli from Nazareth.

My first assignment was harvesting oranges. At half past seven in the morning, together with the two French ladies and two Mexican ladies, I was driven in a truck by the English volunteer through agricultural fields to an orange orchard. On both sides of the sandy path, orange trees lined themselves side by side in neat rows. I learned how to operate a simple machine that enabled me to elevate myself so that I could harvest oranges growing at different heights. While the act of clipping the stalk of an orange is simple, the task of harvesting all the oranges that grow at different heights on a tree requires skills and efficiency. At the end of the workday, at two in the afternoon, I managed to fill up only one crate with the oranges I had harvested.

On the first Saturday I was in the kibbutz, which was also the last Saturday of the month, an outing to Caesarea, a coastal town south of Haifa, was organized for all the volunteers. We walked through huge fields where we came across many shepherd boys with their goats and sheep. After some time, we strolled along the beach and came to the ancient aqueduct built by King Herod around 22 BC to channel water from nearby springs to Caesarea, which had no reliable source of fresh water then. Within Caesarea National Park, we also saw the restored Roman amphitheater, some Byzantine excavations, the citadel, a mosque and some eateries near the rough sea which occasionally sent big sudden splashes to surprise and sabotage tourists. It was an educational outing where history came alive.

A week later, I was assigned to work in the chicken farm of the kibbutz. There were about five long houses wherein the chickens were kept and fed. Before entering the long houses, I had to soak the soles of my shoes in some disinfectant so as not to bring germs from without into the long houses. My job was to randomly select and weigh 150 chickens in each long house: 50 from each end of the long house, and another 50 from the middle section. The average weight of the chicken was then calculated and systematically recorded. Such records enabled the management to track the growth of the chickens in each long house and make suitable adjustments to its poultry farming method.

In addition to weighing the chickens, there was also the morbid task of retrieving the dying and dead chickens from the long houses and disposing them in some oil drums. Apparently, chickens which were dying due to some illness would be attacked and pecked by the stronger ones. Such savagery was truly unthinkable and unimaginable of this seemingly tame and timid creature which flew up in fright whenever I opened the door to the long house. To make sense of such brutality, I reminded myself that chickens are not human beings and therefore lack humanity; moreover, even human beings sometimes exhibit wild and uncontrollable animalism such as the acts of rape and murder.

Apart from harvesting oranges, I was also sometimes sent to harvest avocadoes. By the middle of my second week there, I had made considerable progress in terms of my productivity. Instead of filling only one crate by the end of my first day at the orchard, I could now fill two crates by the end of the workday. Still, I found this job monotonous and boring; the only excitement came from being jerked endlessly by the machine with which I elevated myself to varying heights as I harvested the fruits. To ease my boredom, I often tried to recall old songs and sang to myself while harvesting.

However, life in a kibbutz could be a golden opportunity for self-growth. Regardless of the nature of one's assignment, the time after lunch was usually free for individual pursuits. I used this to interact with volunteers from other countries and learned so much about the world. From the Mexican ladies, I came to know of the two great civilizations of the Mayans and the Aztecs; from a Canadian volunteer, I became acquainted with the problems of farmers in an agricultural community. I also read whenever I picked up a book or a magazine that interested me, such as one by the American poet Robert Frost on poetry, and an article entitled 'A Walk Across

America' that captured a couple's two-and-a half-year walk from New Orleans, where they were married, to Florence in Oregon. Such readings greatly made up for the lack of intellectual stimulation in mundane jobs like harvesting fruits. In addition, I also spent time sketching, playing tennis and cycling within and without the kibbutz with other volunteers, and writing to family and friends to educate them about the existence and purpose of kibbutzim in Israel.

My three weeks in Kibbutz Nirim also taught me a great deal about Jewish history and culture. In my first week there, I had the privilege to witness a Jewish wedding that was conducted under a mobile canopy supported by four poles manually held by four attendants at the wedding ceremony. This canopy, known as chuppah, symbolizes the home that the new couple will build together. Towards the end of my second week there, Moshe, a Jewish resident in the kibbutz came to talk to all the volunteers about the significance of Passover, or Pesach, one of the key events in the Jewish calendar. For the Jews, the event means three things: the exodus of Moses and the people of Israel out of Egypt into the Promised Land; a time of harvest; and the arrival of spring. Just before I left the kibbutz, I had the joy of participating in the eve of Passover celebration, where young and old gathered to dance; I also witnessed the symbolic harvesting ceremony held on the Passover day itself.

My understanding of the way a kibbutz functions was also shaped by my interaction with Rinat, the co-ordinator of foreign volunteers in the kibbutz. She was sincere and friendly and took much effort to explain the volunteer scheme to me. When asked which kind of life she preferred—life in a kibbutz or life in a city, she chose the former. In her explanation, I could detect a sense of contentment in life, one that is often lacking in city-dwellers. Two days before I left the kibbutz, after settling some bills for drinks, I followed Rinat to the children's house. Like all traditional kibbutzim, children in this kibbutz were raised communally by qualified teachers and childcare givers.

Rinat and her husband Dani visited their two young children everyday to spend time and cultivate relationship with them. On that particular day, all parents and their children gathered for a Passover celebration, during which the children were told the story of Moses bringing the people of Israel out of Egypt. In my interaction with Dani, I learned that children who are raised in kibbutzim tend to be more creative, mature and independent. In my mind, I could see the benefits of raising children communally but not having had any prior exposure to this method, I was not immediately convinced that this is a superior way to raise children. Still, I was grateful for having been introduced to another way of raising the next generation; my mind was broadened.

The three weeks in Kibbutz Nirim had enabled me to think and process much about the ideals upon which kibbutzim are based. While I was inclined to endorse the values behind the establishment of such communities, I knew that my young and restless soul could not settle in one for long. I consider this a scheme more suitable for the elderly folks who have seen and explored much of the world and have consequently felt a sense of disgust towards its values, and thus want to abjure forever the materialism embedded in it. But I respect the young adults who voluntarily choose to reside in one. They are a special breed who can make the ideals of kibbutzim come alive.

As for me, I was ready to leave the kibbutz and explore the land of Israel.

My exploration of the Holy Land in the next ten days had the effect of drawing me closer to God. In the Old City of Jerusalem, which is divided into four quarters –Jewish, Christian, Muslim and Armenian, I saw the mingling of religions and beliefs, a peaceful co-existence of people garbed in their traditional garments and religious habits. As I walked through the narrow alleys, I came across many places of worship -- synagogues, churches and mosques, and shops selling religious artifacts such as prayer shawls, rosaries, and ceramics. These places of worship are literally within walking distance from one another, each distinct and separate. However, the same cannot be said of the Dome of the Rock, the octagonal centre-piece of the Old City.

The rock over which the present shrine was built holds significance for both Jews and Muslims. For the former, the rock is believed to be the place where Abraham sacrificed his son Isaac; for the latter, it is traditionally believed that the Prophet Muhammad, founder of Islam, ascended into heaven from the site. I also visited the nearby Wailing Wall where many orthodox Jews in their traditional black garments slipped pieces of their written prayer into the crevices of the wall, believing that their God would hear them and answer them. There was so much religiosity displayed within the Old City. I had so much to learn through my reading of Jerusalem and the different faiths represented in this city; at the same time, I had doubts about the veracity of these faiths.

On Good Friday, I visited Church of the Holy Sepulchre within the Old City. Built in the fourth century, the church is believed to contain two of the holiest sites in Christianity: the site of Jesus' crucifixion and the site of Jesus' empty tomb, where he resurrected. I witnessed endless streams of faithful pilgrims filing in and out of the church, and penned in my diary:

> 'It is amazing how faith can drive people to incredible madness. Thousands of Christians swarm and invade this church, every corner of it. They sit in collective hope, in feverish faith. Especially the old folks, they seem miserable and forlorn, and I sense that they want to rise above this despair through their persistence in an altogether unfamiliar faith, one they would like to believe in but know not very much about.'

For some reason, I walked into the same church again the following morning, but my conscience would not allow me to linger. In my diary, I wrote:

> 'I came out. I don't want to be a part of this madness again, to be one of them, lost in faith. I feel like an intruder, an assailant of this whole concern of faith and devotion. If He really exists, and these people are in the midst of their prayers and praises for Him, what rights do I have, being a doubter, to be a part of them? … To take photos of the holy ceremony is to disrespect the sanctity of the occasion.'

On Easter Sunday, I went to visit Church of the Nativity in Bethlehem, about an hour bus ride from Jerusalem. Within the church is a small grotto where it is believed Jesus was born. On the floor of the grotto is a silver star, supposedly the spot where baby Jesus had lain. I saw many pilgrims kneeling down, bending over to kiss the star, and wondered if that was the appropriate way to show respect. My thought was captured in a short poem I wrote then:

'Behold!
The silver star of the Church of the Nativity,
On which many lips in wondrous faith seal,
And even more curious flashes try to steal.
Why?
If this be the actual birthplace of Christ,
Let your eyes see and minds acknowledge,
And not your impurities its surface tarnish.'

Back in Jerusalem, I was drawn to visit the Garden of Gethsemane at the foot of the Mount of Olives where Jesus agonized over his impending death and prayed in his final hours before his crucifixion. On a slab of stone in the garden, I found this inscription: 'O My Father, if it be possible, let this cup pass from me; nevertheless, not my will, but yours be done. Matthew 26/39'. These were words of surrender uttered by Jesus to God the Father, and they inspired me to entrust my fears to God. In my diary, I wrote: 'My Father, I do not understand You, but I trust You.'

Wanting to have an aerial view of the Old City, I climbed up the Mount of Olives. Indeed, the panoramic view of Jerusalem up on the hill was breathtaking. I could see the Dome of the Rock and the entire walled city beneath my eyes. The cars and buses plying the roads outside the old city walls looked like colored ants crawling persistently alongside the walls. As I was admiring the beauty of it all, a seven-year-old boy came to talk to me. Out of friendliness and adoration for small children, I befriended him and took a photo of him. He plucked some olive leaves for me and offered to show me the way to a nearby church. I thought he was extremely kind until with an outstretched palm, he asked me for some money. I handed him 20 agorot (equivalent to cents), but with perfect English, he told me, "Believe me, this is nothing. Give me more." For some reason, I satisfied his wish and gave him another shekel (equivalent to a dollar). In my mind, I reasoned that he had been corrupted by the money that tourists brought to this place; in my heart, I wished that fewer tourists would come here to further corrupt him and other children of his age.

Apart from Jerusalem, I also visited other historical sites in the vicinity such as the Dead Sea at En Gedi and Masada near the southern end of the Dead Sea. Although the Dead Sea is not prominently featured in the Bible, ancient Jewish religious scrolls were found in the vicinity of Qumran near the Dead Sea in the late 1940s. These ancient scrolls bear witness to the accuracy of some parts of the Old Testament in the Bible. For most tourists, however, it is not for this reason that they flock to the Dead Sea; they come for health reasons. It is said that the heavy salt and magnesium content in the water can improve the elasticity of one's skin; the Dead Sea mud when applied to one's body is also able to remove impurities and relieve pain caused by inflammation.[1]

I floated in the Dead Sea for a while but did not apply the black mud on my body as I wanted to spend some time at Masada further south before returning to Jerusalem in the late afternoon. Masada is an ancient fortification built by Herod the Great between 37 and 31 BC on top of an isolated rock plateau. I bought a guidebook on Masada and learned about the First Jewish-Roman War which culminated in the destruction of the city of Jerusalem and its Temple in AD 70, and the capture of the fortress of Masada in AD 73.

My sightseeing in Israel also brought me to the historic town of Jericho and the vicinity of the Sea of Galilee in the north where Jesus moved about in the early days of His ministry. In Jericho, I saw the excavations of the remains of the wall of Jericho, made famous by the story of Joshua and his men marching around the city wall for seven days: 'On the seventh day, they got up at daybreak and marched around the city seven times in the usual manner, except that on that day they circled the city seven times... When the trumpets sounded, the people shouted, and at the sound of the trumpet, when the people gave a loud shout, the wall collapsed; so every man charged straight in, and they took the city.'[2]

I also joined a day tour at Tiberias, a city on the western shore of the Sea of Galilee. Among the places I visited were the Golan Heights with Mount Hermon in

---

[1] Retrieved from https://www.healthline.com/health/dead-sea-mud#improves-psoriasis

[2] From the book of Joshua, chapter 6, verses 15 and 20, in the Old Testament.

the background; an Israeli–Lebanon border checkpoint manned by United Nations soldiers; the Banias spring at the foot of Mount Hermon; the Mount of the Beatitudes, where Jesus delivered His sermon known as The Beatitudes, and where I noted the inscription: 'Blessed are the peacemakers for they shall be called the children of God. Matthew 5/9'; and the Church of Heptapegon, wherein I noted the following inscription: 'Jesus said, Bring the five loaves and two fishes hither to Me. And they did all eat and were filled. Matthew 14/18+20'. That was the place Jesus fed five thousand people with five loaves of bread and two fish, and one could see the mosaic of fish and bread on the church floor. The visit to such places where Jesus had been to and performed miracles really piqued my interest to know more about the life story of Jesus. I was determined to read more about Jesus after this trip.

The highlight of my last day in Israel was a visit to the Museum of the Jewish Diaspora located within Tel Aviv University. I immersed myself in understanding the dispersion of the Jewish people; I scrutinized the exhibits and the captions and copied the following in my diary:

> 'This is the story of a people which was scattered over all the world and yet remained a single family; a nation which time and again was doomed to destruction and yet, out of the ruins rose to new life.'

> 'Assyrians, Babylonians and Romans conquered the land and drove the Jews into exile but the Jewish nation persisted.'

'The Jews practiced circumcision in joy and in peril throughout the generations.'

'The Jewish family put the child's education above everything.'

'In the year 1933, Adolf Hitler came into power in Germany. In his time, the Germans and their accomplices murdered 6 million Jews, among them a million and a half Jewish children. Imprisoned in ghettoes, the victims fought desperately for their lives, while the world stood by in silence.'

'Belief in the one God and the sanctity of human life are the supreme values of the Jewish religion. The Torah and its commandments embrace man's total life experience. After the destruction of the Second Temple, the synagogue represented Jewish continuity.'

'The story of the interaction between the Jews and their changing environments is a continuous drama of settlement and expulsion, disaster and recovery.'

The visit to this museum taught me so much about the history of the Jews, how resilient and indestructible they are. To a large extent, their ability to endure and survive through centuries of persecutions has to do with their steadfast practice of their religion, Judaism, and their allegiance to their God.

Such an understanding of the Jewish religion prepared me for the unexpected crowning experience of my month-long sojourn in this country. After spending many hours in the museum, I was strolling quietly by myself in a park outside the university when a middle-aged man approached me and shared his life experience at length with me. As a Jew growing up in the United States, he had just recently migrated to Israel to settle there. A series of dreams in which he heard a divine voice calling him to return to the land of his ancestors, and some circumstances which confirmed that it was indeed the voice of God, prompted him to make the big move.

At the end of his narration, he told me that my visit to Israel was not coincidental, but that God had meant it as a way for me to know Him better. I did not argue with him. Indeed, my visit to the Holy Land had enhanced my understanding of God; moreover, this man's parting words that my trip was not a coincidence complemented the dream my friend Selvam gave me before my departure, that God would be the shepherd guiding me along this trip.

I had learned so much about Israel, about the Jewish people, and about God. On this trip, God had shown me great and unsearchable truths about the Bible. I was determined to learn more upon my return to Loughborough.

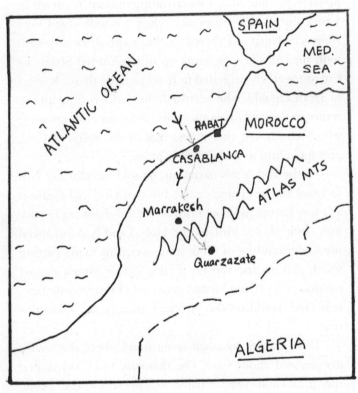

Map 3 : Morocco

CHAPTER 4

Experiencing God in Morocco

"The desert and the parched land will be glad; the wilderness will rejoice and blossom. Like the crocus, it will burst into bloom; it will rejoice greatly and shout for joy."

Isaiah 35:1-2a

I returned to my university on Sunday, 26th April 1987 afternoon, a day before the new and final term began. Apart from moving boxes of my belongings from the storeroom back to my own room, I had to do the laundry arising from my one month in Israel. But it was a joy to be back in Loughborough, as I was looking forward to receiving and reading letters from family and friends that had arrived in the last five weeks (emails were not commonly used at that time). I was eager to write and share with them my experiences in Israel.

As a result of my travels in Israel, I became more interested to read the Bible. Soon after settling down to my weekly routine, I started joining the Navigators on campus, a Christian ministry that helps seekers and new believers know Christ and to grow in their knowledge of the Bible. I would occasionally join their early morning prayer meetings though I did not understand much of the Bible, especially readings taken from the Old Testament. Indeed, I became so absorbed in reading the Bible and Christian books that I did not prepare much for my examinations in mid-June. After the examinations, I feared the prospect of failing some subjects. However, my fears were unfounded; I thanked God that overall, I managed a second-lower class. The greater consolation was that results from the first year were not counted towards the overall degree.

My involvement with the Navigators led me to sign up for a ten-day Navigators' Camp in Wales in early July 1987. Apart from wanting to learn more about God, I was excited at the prospect of seeing Wales, and participating in the many outdoor activities lined up for the camp. Indeed, the program for the camp was more than what I could ask for; we went caving, canoeing, hiking, rock climbing, abseiling and sailing, in addition to many fun-filled games. There were also talks about God, sin, and our need for God, all of which I found meaningful.

On one of the evenings, all the groups were supposed to dramatize a passage from the Bible given to them. In my group, I played the role of Jesus being tempted by the devil after fasting forty days and forty nights,[3] and wanting to immerse myself in the role, I fasted prior to the performance. As a matter of fact, I did feel physically weak

---

[3]   The story is found in the Gospel of Matthew, chapter 4, verses 1-11.

but spiritually strengthened during the dramatization. (Months later, I was informed by someone from the Navigators that my portrayal of Jesus was very real.) In the middle of the camp was a presentation by a mission organization. I learned about bringing the gospel of Christ to other nations; in particular, I was challenged to pray and consider joining a mission trip to Morocco from late July to early August that year.

Two days after the camp in Wales, I confirmed my participation in the mission trip to Morocco. However, there were a few important matters to settle: a visa to enter Morocco, several mandatory vaccinations before the trip, and the availability of air-tickets. The most pressing and tricky one was to secure a visa from the Moroccan embassy in London. Due to some reason, the embassy would be shut the week after the camp, and that left me with only three days to apply and procure a valid visa before the trip itself. Given the situation, I could only pray and leave the matter in God's hand. As it turned out, the mission organization was able to contact someone to offer me free lodging while I was awaiting my visa in London, which was a great help financially. As for the vaccinations, I had them done in Loughborough prior to travelling down to London. I also bought a pocket-sized Bible for my trip to Morocco, which became my constant companion on many other trips.

The journey from Heathrow Airport to the house in Marrakesh where we were to spend the next few nights took about seven hours. The plane stopped at Tangier (a coastal city in the north) and then Casablanca (another coastal city further south) where we transferred to a domestic flight to Marrakesh. Upon touching down at Marrakesh, we were greeted by some personnel from the organization and driven to a house which also acted as the headquarters. Once there, we were served tea and coffee together with some broken pieces of biscuits, before being given a briefing about the facilities and the program.

The facilities in this house were rather basic. The sleeping area reserved for the nine of us measured approximately six by three metres. We were to use our own camping mats and sleeping bags which were standard packing items in the equipment list given to us before the trip. The alternative was to sleep on the veranda on the roof top, which some of us did. As for shower, each of us was permitted to use only one bucket of water a day; we were taught to recycle the water. First, one should fill a pail, punctured with a few holes at the bottom, with water and hang it on a hook above; then one should stand or sit in a bigger pail beneath the pail dripping with water to wash oneself, so that the used water can be recycled. Repeatedly, we were told that water was scarce in that part of the country and that it should be conserved at all times.

The first week was spent acclimatizing to the hot and dry weather, learning more about the Moroccan culture and religion, and of course the basics of the Arabic language. There was also the daily sharing of the word of God from the Bible, from which we learned more about God and through which we reflected on His higher purpose for each one of us, including the local Moroccans. We also took walks in the surrounding villages and gained deeper insights into the local culture and practices. Somehow, the huge masses of mountains surrounding the villages reminded me of Golan Heights and the densely-packed stone and clay houses, the refugee camps in the West Bank of Israel.

I found my spirits swinging to extremities according to the weather conditions. When the scorching heat burned in the middle of the day, I fumed with irritation within; when the wind blew across the mountain ranges, I rejoiced in the refreshment it brought to this vast and beautiful land. Once in the middle of the day, a sandstorm descended upon us and the entire skyline was covered by a pervasive layer of brownness. Standing out in the open, we could hardly open our eyes wide, yet we did not wish to go indoors: the room was simply too warm at that time of the day, even if claustrophobia was absent. I learned to accept the external conditions that cannot be changed; this changed me, internally.

Our walks around the villages usually happened around the late afternoon or dusk when the heat was more bearable. After one of these walks, I reminisced and wrote in my diary:

> 'The walk to the mountain ridge was good. It was a rare sight: a view of unequalled beauty. Sincerely, it would be difficult to describe the scenery and yet do it justice. Huge plains with undulating slopes perfected only by nature, by wind. And treading slowly but surely, the donkeys humbly brought their owners' supplies to their destinations. It is like God faithfully leading us to His kingdom – a long and perhaps very gradual process, but nonetheless a promise that would be fulfilled eventually. And I thought of these simple and friendly villagers, so unspoiled and untainted by materialism

and modernization, living so far and remote in their hiding places, searching for the truth of life. But exactly how is God's power and truth going to reach them and touch them? I wonder. He alone knows.'

As a young Christian, I also benefited from the many talks based on the teachings in the Bible. After one particular morning devotion, I reflected on the message and reminded myself to be true before God:

'We must constantly remind ourselves of our honesty and sincerity with God. He is not pleased by means of our looks, our outfits, and our boastful deeds. These can only impress earthly beings who have totally or partially forsaken their intimacy with God. Take away that external self, cover, or jacket, and reveal your true naked self which cannot be stripped. Delight in what God has created in you and present yourself in that original form before Him, without pretense, hiddenness and embarrassment. Whatever you do to your fellow men you do onto God; whatever you try to impress your fellow men you try to impress Him, and He is not impressed.'

In the second week, after some acclimatization and armed with some basic knowledge of the Arabic language, we were brought on an overnight trek in the

Atlas Mountains. We carried our backpacks and trekked from one village to another, and along the way met many villagers who were ever willing to direct us and guide us. Despite the initial slow start, we made it to our destination at the end of the day, when I settled down under the stars to write about our journey:

'The beauty of God's creation in the heart of the Atlas Mountains is beyond description. Breathtaking, magnificent, awe-inspiring – these words fall short in giving one a good and justifiable picture of the landscape. Vast endless plains of rocks, stones and sand, all waiting to be conquered; conquered; and yet more to beconquered. We saw what great distances we had covered behind us, and then saw far greater distances ahead of us. Endless. Everlasting. And amidst the dryness, aridness and barrenness springs forth a valley of life, of stone-brick houses and lush green plantations, well-irrigated. The villagers, secluded and isolated in this corner of the world, seem to lead a simple, peaceful and harmonious life, totally undisturbed, unperturbed and unpolluted by the artificiality of modernization. There is a strong communal spirit amongst them, always friendly, helpful and willing to share.'

The two-day-one-night trek was meant as a preparation for our finale, a small-group independent expedition to another more rural city to make connections with the locals and to pray for them. The nine of us were divided into two small teams, each heading to a different city deep within the country. I was grouped with Bel, Christine and Dave and we were sent to explore and acquaint ourselves with Ouarzazate, a city in the middle of a bare plateau south of the Atlas Mountains and one that is often used as an entry point to the desert further south. The journey by bus from Marrakesh to Ouarzazate would take about five hours as the Atlas Mountains separate the two cities, and the bus had to wind its way up and down the steep and treacherous slopes of the mountains.

As a new Christian, I was not sure what I could accomplish on this trip except to learn more about God. However, I was given the task of a peacemaker. Just before our departure to Ouarzazate, a leader of the mission organization spoke to me in private to be God's mediator between Bel and Christine. Though the two had been in the same team for more than a week, they did not get along well; one was too assertive and the other too timid but resentful. In my diary, I implored God:

> 'Give us the right atmosphere, the conducive environment and a peaceful and tranquil state of mind for each one of us tonight. Teach me to be sensitive to either's needs, and put words into my mouth. Help me in your miraculous, loving way to resolve the difference, to ease the tension and to reconcile the two polarities of gentleness and strength. I

believe in your capacity to act, and trust
in your faithfulness.'

God heard the yearning of my heart. After checking
into a campsite at Ouarzazate, the four of us found time to
talk and to get to know one another better. We were able
to share our hearts, our hopes and fears with one another,
and after the sharing to pray for one another. That night,
in my diary, I thanked God profusely:

> 'O faithful God, thank you so much for
> this conversation. Thank you for the
> words you put into my mouth. Thank
> you for that final prompting in Chris'
> heart for her to speak up. And thank you
> for that openness in Bel to see and agree
> with certain points. God, keep working
> in each one of them: teach Bel to be more
> sensitive to other people's feelings and
> give Chris the courage to air her views
> every time she sees the need to do so.
> God, I do want to ask you to give us a
> test through which we can work closely
> together, each having something to
> contribute. God, bring out the finer gifts
> you have given each of us so that we can
> use them to glorify you.'

The next morning, we set off to explore the city of
Ouarzazate, and to acquaint ourselves with its people.
Along the way, we came across many earthen clay
buildings ranging from two to three-storey high, and
small clusters of tall thin palm trees scattered sporadically

along the semi-dirt roads. Small children aged six to ten gathered outside their houses; the boys were playing football while the girls looked on with amusement. It must be school vacation for them as summer months are known to be the hottest. We had the good fortune to befriend a man in his early twenties who knew how to speak English. He, Mohamed, was a student of a hotel and hospitality management school in Marrakesh and was spending his summer vacation at home. Eager to practise his English with us, he invited us to his house where we were served some mint tea, a traditional tea in this country.

We introduced ourselves and made it known that we were in the country to learn more about its culture and religion. That gave us an entry point to ask many questions about his life, his values and beliefs. Naturally, we also shared ours with him. Apart from Mohamed, there were five other ladies in the family: one mother and presumably four other sisters. When we asked for permission to take a photo with all the ladies in the family, they took out a big red carpet with small green diamond shapes on it,[4] and hung it over the parapet wall on the open veranda which acted as the backdrop of the photo. The carpet must be a prized possession of the family which they wanted to show to us. Before we parted ways, we exchanged our addresses, and I promised to send him the photos.[5]

My earlier prayer for God to test our unity was answered in an unexpected way on the last day as we prepared to return to Marrakesh. After a cool and refreshing drink

---

[4] Incidentally, red and green are the colors of the Moroccan flag.

[5] I did send him the photos and we communicated for another three years.

in the early morning, we made our way to the filthy and deserted bus station where we learned that there would not be any bus operating that day. "A national holiday," we were told. Undeterred, we gathered under a shady spot and prayed for God to provide a way out of the situation. Shortly after our prayer, we saw another two men who confirmed once again that no bus would be available that day. Instead they suggested we hire a car and drive all the way back to Marrakesh. However, to do this, we would require a letter of approval from the police since Christine, the only one among us who could drive, did not bring along her driving license. The policeman we approached recommended that we hitch a ride instead from other guests checking out of the campsite that day or, failing which, we could get onto the next bus that evening, arriving at Marrakesh at about midnight.

All things seemed to work against us. By the time we got back to the campsite, all the guests had left; and however hard we tried to convey our desperate situation, the police refused to give us a letter of approval to hire a car. Undaunted by the adversity we were facing and determined to get back to Marrakesh before night fell, we walked down the main road, all set to hitch a ride from any passing vehicles. There and then, we prayed with great faith, constantly reminding ourselves that God would provide a miracle for us.

About ten minutes later, a policeman on a scooter came and informed us that a bus would be coming and heading back to Marrakesh. "What bus?" we asked, surprised and yet overjoyed, and waited in eager, expectant mood. True enough, a few minutes later, an empty bus appeared out of nowhere and we were elated. With limited Arabic, we were not able to find out from the driver and his co-driver why they were heading to Marrakesh; we were able to confirm that it would be going to Marrakesh and we thanked God for answering our prayer.

Much to our delight, the bus journey back to Marrakesh was more than just a ride. About two hours later, as the bus climbed the slopes of the Atlas Mountains, it came to a halt in the middle of the mountain road. Soon, a servant of a house nearby came running out with a big carpet which he laid under a spreading tree nearby. Judging by the shadows cast on the ground, it must be around noon time then. Together with the two local drivers, we were invited to take a rest under the coolness of the spreading tree, while the servant went back to the house and emerged again with a water jug (with water for us to wash hands), a kettle, teacups, and some Moroccan delicacies. Finally, the owner of the house appeared with his two children, a boy of about twelve and a girl of about six. Their immaculately clean attire contrasted with the sand and dirt around them and reflected their middle-class status. We could not communicate much with them but simply smiled and thanked them for their hospitality. Apparently, hospitality towards strangers is one of the hallmarks of Moroccans,[6] whether it be in the cities or up in the mountains.

Our last morning in Marrakesh was spent on team debriefing and personal reflection. As I reflected on the past two weeks in Morocco, I was thankful for the lovely people I met: leaders of the mission organization, team

---

[6]   Morocco is the third most welcoming country in the world according to a 2013 survey done by World Economic Forum, measuring the quality of being warm and welcoming to strangers. Retrieved from https://friendlymorocco.com/culture/moroccan-hospitality/

members, and even the locals. In my diary, I wrote a short letter of gratitude to God:

> 'Thank you, God, for all these lovely people. They are indeed a great help and encouragement to me. I have grown and matured through them, and have certainly come to know you better. Never mind that I cannot see you physically; I believe that we will meet someday and that you will shower me with much more blessings and love. And though I may have to carry the burden of my anxiety sometimes, I know that eventually I will have the taste of paradise, of happiness, freewill and loving kindness in abundance.'

We were given an afternoon to wander in the old historic part of town called Medina with its high stone walls. It resembles somewhat the Old City of Jerusalem except that the wares sold in it were typically Moroccan such as silverware, handicrafts, textile and souvenirs. Here and there, donkeys were seen transporting goods from one cobblestone lane to another, while little children played on their own, oblivious to the donkeys and human traffic flowing around them. I wove in and out of the narrow lanes, capturing the unique scenes with my camera and avoiding those who asked to be paid if they were photographed. As I walked through the maze, I also set my eyes on some interesting souvenirs from this land; finally, I settled on a blue and white Moroccan rug, a multi-colored prayer mat, and a silver Moroccan teapot -- to remind me of the hospitality of the locals.

I left Marrakesh with a lot to thank God for. While transiting and waiting in Casablanca airport for our international flight back to London, my heart was teeming with excitement and gratitude towards God, and words of lyrical beauty just flowed out spontaneously in my diary in two distinct parts:

Part I

From time immemorial, even before the creation of the world,
You have chosen me and known me, my temperament and my being;
Such was the extent of our relationship. But the ignorant me,
The stubborn self blinded by the dazzling lights of the world,
Had thought myself sufficient, in strength and in thought,
To survive my very own existence, when all the while
You were there guiding my every step, pulling me up when I fell,
And giving me that extra push when my own energy failed me.

O faithful, faithful friend!
How can I adequately thank thee and praise thee,
Doing thee justice for whatever thou have done for me,
Knowing by my own words and power, limited,
I will surely fall short in exalting thy perfection.

Part II

'Your oceans wide and deep,
Wave-like mountains rising and ebbing,
Rock, sand, dust and air, pervasive as the heat,
Bordered and blanketed this land which now I leave
(behind),
Knowing and remembering in her I grew, to You I
closer drew.

What love, what joy, what company!
To touch and to be touched, that sensation, that spirit,
Bubbling with excitement, high, higher than cloud nine,
Building up to that unutterable silence, perturbed
Only by an overwhelming feeling of gladness and
deep joy.

My friend, all my soul rejoice with thee!
Thou are exalted high above all the earth,
Now, then, forever and evermore.'

I departed from Morocco in a plane and my spirit
was soaring above cloud nine. I had experienced deep
intimacy and friendship with God and wandered what
He would have me do for the rest of my summer vacation.

I returned to Singapore in mid-August 1987 and spent
about a month with my family and friends. As a result
of my participation in the trip to Morocco, my name
and contact numbers were forwarded to two English
ladies, Sarah and Sue, serving full-time with the same
mission organization. They were in Singapore then and
contacted me one day, inviting me to join them for a
ten-day exploration of Java in Indonesia. We flew into

Jakarta, and travelled to Semarang, Yogyakarta, Malang and Jombang, before returning to Jakarta. Along the way, we met many local Christians and pastors as well as foreign missionaries, and visited some local Bible schools which not only taught their students the word of God but also practical farming skills, with which they could earn a living. At the end of the trip, Sarah, the team leader, wrote me a letter to encourage me to continue to seek God and to grow in Him.

Indeed, I had grown much spiritually this summer but I needed further grounding in the word of God.

Map 4 : Italy

CHAPTER 5

Waxing Poetic in Italy

"… I have filled him with the Spirit of God, with wisdom, with understanding, with knowledge and with all kinds of skills—to make artistic designs for work in gold, silver and bronze, to cut and set stones, to work in wood, and to engage in all kinds of crafts."

Exodus 31:2-5

In early October 1987, I found myself back in England and her gentility. As I started my second year in Loughborough University, I disciplined and applied myself not only to academic pursuits and sports but also to spiritual growth. To achieve the latter, I joined a weekly Navigators' Bible study through which I learned much about God's word and His character. I was thankful to have a faithful Bible study leader who without fail turned up weekly at my hall of residence to guide me in the study. Over time, I cultivated the habit of reading God's word every morning and evening before bedtime, hearing God's voice and praying to Him. It is a discipline that has guided me through life's many difficult decisions, and one that I still practise and maintain today.

God speaks when one reads the Bible with the guidance of the Holy Spirit. One distinct example of God speaking to me was an incident in late autumn that year. I had earlier in the year come across an Operation Raleigh[7] poster in a London underground station and had applied to join the expedition. However, to go on an expedition, one had to go through a selection weekend and be selected. In a letter from the organization, I was invited to participate in a selection weekend at a meeting point in the suburbs of Oxford on a Saturday morning.[8] To make it there on time, it meant that I had to travel to Oxford on a Friday night. But where was I to spend the night in Oxford? I had no idea. I did not wish to spend money on accommodation in Oxford in addition to the coach fare I had to pay.

That particular Friday morning, as I was reading God's word from Genesis 46: 1-4, God's reassurance to Jacob, "I am God, the God of your father. Do not be afraid to go down to Egypt..." spoke to me. Instantly, I felt deep within me that God was asking me not to worry about where I would be spending the night at Oxford. That evening, with His peace, I boarded a National Express coach that was passing through Loughborough on its way to Oxford, not knowing where I would lay my head upon arrival. To my surprise and sheer delight, I met a

---

[7] Launched by Britain's Prince Charles, Operation Raleigh is an ambitious, four-year scientific and archaeological expedition that will involve some 4,000 young men and women from varied backgrounds and cultures.

[8] I was selected that weekend and went on an expedition to Chile in 1991. Read chapters 13 and 14.

familiar face on the coach: a fellow Singaporean who was studying in Oxford but with whom I had not kept in contact. Without me asking, he offered to put me up in his room for the night. In my heart, I shouted, "Hallelujah!" This incident contributed in no small amount to my faith in God.

The winter vacation of December 1987 saw me remaining in Loughborough. For the first time since I started university, I did not travel out of England during a vacation. I suppose the chief reason must be the many academic assignments I had to complete during that vacation; also, I wanted to save some money for the Easter vacation in March 1988. In addition, by this time, Loughborough had become a second home to me and I did not mind lingering in it for some weeks. This feeling of home was due in large part to the warmth shown me by three elderly Christian couples in this town: the Robertsons, the Crowhursts, and the Booklesses. They were love and wisdom personified; after a visit to any of the couples, I would be encouraged to love others and to know God more.

My initial plan for the Easter vacation was to visit some parts of Turkey and Greece, the places the apostle Paul in the New Testament had been to. It was my intention to retrace the footsteps of the apostle and to experience the power of the same God that was with him on his missionary journeys. However, my study of the English Renaissance literature covering writers such as Sir Thomas More (1478-1535), Ben Johnson (1572-1637), William Shakespeare (1564-1616), Christopher Marlowe (1564-1593), and John Milton (1608-1674) had the effect of drawing me to visit Italy, the birthplace of the Renaissance movement. In addition, apart from literature, I was also interested to see the masterpieces of famous artists such as Leonardo da Vinci, Botticelli, and Michelangelo. In the end, art and literature held sway over biblical history. Towards the end of the term in early March, I found myself lugging heaps of books on Italy from the university library to my room; I told myself that I was studying for three degrees in this university: English, Physical Education, and Travelling!

The flight from London to Venice on 20 March 1988 was exhilarating. The plane flew across the Alps. Through the window next to my seat, I saw layers of mountains painted in pockets of white, each different in form and yet collectively, they were a picture of fairyland, a wintry landscape. I imagined myself to have gained divine status by virtue of my elevated position; as I looked down, the mighty mountains seemed miniscule to me. But this feeling did not last a long time. Soon after that, the plane touched down at Venice airport, and I began to regain human perspective of things. I boarded an airport bus that brought me straight to the bus station on Venice island, where I met an Iranian by the name of Javad who was also travelling solo.

Javad and I found a friend in each other immediately and decided to see Venice together, even sharing a room in Hotel Bartolomeo in order to save cost. We sauntered to Saint Mark's Square and basked in the joy of being in Venice on a beautiful afternoon in spring. There were crowds of people sitting or standing on this big square, some feeding pigeons, the sight of which reminded me of Trafalgar Square in London. We climbed the stairs of Saint Mark's Basilica and visited the upper galleries from which we had a bird's eye view of the entire square and noticed the long shadows of the people cast on the ground by the late afternoon sun. Nearby, gondolas lined the pier, waiting for passengers to pay and board. We ambled along the pier, soaking in the festive atmosphere and appreciating the warm glow of the red spherical sun setting on the far horizon.

In the evening, I wrote a postcard to my Singaporean friends back in Loughborough to share with them my impressions of Venice:

> 'The merchants of Venice are really making good money. So much charm has Venice to offer to tourists that even at this time of the year, the city is packed with travelers from all over the world, including at least one from Singapore. Her waterways are her streets, and her boats and gondolas her lorries and cars; here and there, one gets a view from a bridge which is narrow but revealing in the very characteristics of this old and enchanting city. Like a love affair which can be narrated but not felt in the same intensity and passion, so I am sure that all forms and manners of writing and describing will never convey the heightened joy and inner delight of my heart. But perhaps you can be that much closer in your imagination when I tell you that there are seagulls flying over and engulfing this island. Venice--the beauty of God's creation. Highly recommended.'

The next morning, we walked to the nearby majestic Rialto Bridge, the oldest bridge spanning the Grand Canal in Venice. Both the bridge and the areas around it were teeming with activities of buying and selling. Even Shylock, the Jew in the Shakespearean play, *The Merchant of Venice*, refers to Rialto as an area of bustling trade. We saw throngs of tourists crossing the bridge in both directions, occasionally stopping to browse the souvenirs in the shops and at the mobile stalls set up in front of them; we also explored the narrow alleys further away from the Grand Canal where typically the distance between one three-storey building to another is about five metres or less. The proximity even allowed some residents to secure wires or ropes from one building to another, on which they hung their laundry. It was truly a sight of extreme creativity and claustrophobia.

Javad and I parted ways probably in the late morning. He was on his way back to Iran while I was going to travel south to Rome. Though our time together was short, I nevertheless thanked God for the opportunity to meet him. We exchanged addresses and promised to keep in touch.[9] That evening, I recorded in my diary: 'I am writing this so as to remember to pray for Javad, the resourceful Iranian I met in Venice. Praise God for the opportunity to share Jesus Christ with him, and I would like to pray for God's holy touch upon him as he reads the New Testament I gave him as a gift.'[10] Being on a shoestring budget and with nobody to share the cost of a room in this expensive

---

[9] We did keep in touch through letters. In fact, he came to visit me in England in Feb, 1990.

[10] After the mission trip in Morocco, I learned to pack some pocket Bibles as gifts which I can give to others during my travels.

city, I found myself resorting to spend the night at Venice railway station. In the middle of the night, I felt somebody fiddle with the upper pocket of my denim jacket, but when I opened my eyes, I saw nobody around me except that the string on my Silva compass which was attached to my denim jacket had been snapped. The peril of sleeping overnight alone in a railway station!

My first stop after Venice was Padua, claimed to be the oldest city in northern Italy. Most tourists come here to visit the Scrovegni Chapel wherein they could see the frescoes, painted by Giotto between 1303 and 1305, which narrate the life story of the Virgin Mary and Christ. By then, having read the gospel of Matthew, I was quite familiar with the events that led to the birth, death and resurrection of Jesus Christ and could understand the portrayal of Christ in the frescoes. I also visited the Basilica of St. Anthony, and strolled around the picturesque open-air markets of Piazza delle Erbe (Square of the Herbs) and Piazza della Frutta (Square of Fruit) on both sides of the massive 13th-century Palazzo della Ragione (Law Courts). To me, this city had a peaceful and quiet charm, but it was lacking in youthful energy and vitality.

My experience in the next city, Bologna, proved to be different. Soon after my arrival in this city by train, I met three young music students probably in their early twenties. One of them, Patrizia, could speak English well and it was mainly through her that I introduced myself to the group. Upon hearing that I was travelling solo in Italy on a shoestring budget, they made arrangement for me to spend a night at a students' apartment in their university. They also gave me some suggestions regarding the places of interest that I could explore in Bologna. I walked to the main square in the city centre, Maggiore Square, surrounded by medieval and Renaissance buildings and lined with cafes and street musicians, and visited the nearby Two Towers, a symbolic landmark of the city built by noble families in the 12th century. I thanked God for these three angels who not only housed me and pointed me to some of the best sites in the city but also invited me to attend their final concert rehearsal that evening, which I gladly accepted.

 To me, that invitation to see the musicians rehearse was an offer to have a rare glimpse into their private world, and one that would not come by easily for any foreign visitors to the country. I rejoiced in the privilege but a part of me also questioned if my presence was a kind of intrusion into their lives. In my diary, I expressed the tension within:

> 'I suddenly found myself thrown into the private world of these budding musicians of Italy. Oh, to think of this moment in life, a brief yet precious glimpse of the lifestyle of these young musicians, this, this must be an experience of a lifetime, an education. I thank God for the opportunity, but I confess I know not how I should bring it to an end—a memorable end. There is a tension of emotions straining inside me. I appreciate the hospitality of these people, but I also feel I am imposing myself on them, in their private world. And this very suspicion of intrusion makes me want to leave instantly. Still, I must treat the matter with care and consideration; it

must be a farewell to be remembered and
treasured. God, please guide me in this.'

I was grateful to God for this brief stop at Bologna
but I was also eager to move on to Florence, the city most
famous for its Renaissance art and culture. As I bade
farewell to the musicians and travelled in a train towards
Florence, their music and humanity reverberated in my
mind, thrilling my every sensation. Deep in my heart, I
knew I would keep in touch with Patrizia and share my
onward travels in Italy with her.[11]

My first day in Florence was, to say the least, most
magical and fairytale-like. After spending a night at the
railway station in order to save money on accommodation,
I checked into a hostel the next morning. I was ready
to visit the museums and art galleries in Florence but
instead found myself travelling with a German girl to Pisa
(to see the Leaning Tower) and the beach nearby. The
conversation for that day was recorded in the following
poem:[12]

Paradise Restored

By Chance or Fate to this hostel I came,
And found Daniela eating her breakfast.

---

[11] I did write to Patrizia when I returned to Loughborough,
and we kept in touch for a few more years.

[12] The poem, Paradise Restored, written mostly in iambic
pentameter, was started at Piazzale Michelangelo in
Florence and later polished and lengthened through three
almost sleepless nights back in Loughborough, and then
submitted as part of my creative writing portfolio to
Loughborough University for grading.

That, she put aside, and offered me help,
Which by and by struck we a sweet accord,
And decided to travel together.

  To the beach we went, shoes in hands, and bags
Of food, and tales each to the other told:
She for her part was sad, (jilted of late
By he whose heart she sought,) and desirous
Of love, burnt with pain and emotion deep,
Seeking to be touched, and kissed, and embraced:
The want that is in all women to live.

  To which I advised that God all her needs
Could meet in fullness, and joy, abundance,
And Man no God is but an instrument
With whom to serve God better than before.

  But with anguish my words she retorted:
The God who created Adam and Eve,
Who tempted them with the Forbidden Tree,
And then punished them, was an unjust God,
Completely void of love, compassion naught,
To Him she could not turn, let alone serve.

  I bade her consider the Sin of Man,
Who chose out of Freewill to disobey
His higher command, but lowly submit
To a bent Rib,[13] warped, and tampered with
The ire of God, not so unjust, but just.

  Her fire yet unquenched, she refuted:
A God of love hath not the need to withhold
An Apple Tree -- He creates, He bestows;
Freely gotten, freely given; with love
He hath not need the pledge of faith from Man.

---

[13] It refers to Eve according to the creation story found in
Genesis 2:22.

True love, said I, cometh with Discipline,
Which left unused, unsung, un-companied,
Is like a bride divorced from her bridegroom,
She cannot happy be, it must be so:
One without the other is unwholesome,
With love He needs include due Discipline.

But still her mind would not accept this truth,
Too harsh, she said His Cane, too stern His Love,
That He, invisible, intangible,
Could never physically touch her soul,
That longed for a sensual, human embrace,
That has been searching, waiting, ten ripe years,
For one who truly loves, and now her heart
Hath turned into a sickened rose, that soon
With woe and pain would die a gruesome death.

Cheer up! I heartened her to suspect not
The good and prosperous plans God hath made
For all His children, nor leave, nor forsake,
Even, constant, and everlasting be.

Upon this high exaltation of God,
She heaved a heavy sigh, and shook her head,
Remarked that I had not her understood,
Her inner self, of body, mind, and soul.

On which I pondered, deliberated,
And prayed for Wisdom, which came that instant
As sudden as a gushing wind: embraced
And kissed, her body and her lips, quite numbed
With shock and mix'd delight, she stared at me,
And asked for what reason I did that deed,
And quickly added, my sincerity,
Not so necessity, should prompt that kiss.

O Wisdom! Wisdom never known before,
That moment flow'd from system deep within

To still, silence, and sing of human praise:
I said the kiss I gave at best remained,
In time to come, a passing memory.
But not the love of God if felt within,
The joy is lasting, always present, real,
And fades not, neither time, nor circumstance,
Hath toll upon its Beauty – still, serene.

    I scarce had known the glorious words I spoke,
When angels high above rejoiced, rejoiced,
And sang a song so sweet methought it fit
To charm Eros to his love-sick Psyche.

    When next I found my feet in sand buried,
The sun had merged the sea. It came to mind:
A Spirit in the air had swung her up,
And led her walking, hand in hand, with me.

The next morning, against my urge to spend more time with Daniela, I roamed the streets of Florence by myself to appreciate this city of art. Like most tourists, I headed towards Piazza della Signoria, a great square dominated by the imposing Palazzo Vecchio which has for centuries been a focal point of Florentine political and civic life. There were sculptures all around the square, including a fountain featuring a gigantic Neptune, the Roman god of waters and seas. Bicycles, cars and horse-drawn carriages were jostling for space on the narrow roads. However, the pace of life was leisurely and unhurried; here and there, groups of young people were sitting along the pavements, basking in the gentle morning sunshine while little children with food in hand were seen feeding the pigeons that had gathered around them. Round a corner, I saw street artists at work, busy sketching the portraits of their patrons while on-lookers smiled and nodded their heads in approval, complimenting the artists for their skills.

My exploration of the city brought me further south to the famous bridge synonymous with Florence, Ponte Vecchio. A picturesque medieval stone bridge with Roman origins, it was lined with jewelry and souvenir shops. In the middle of the bridge stood the bust of the great Florentine sculptor and master goldsmith, Benvenuto Cellini. Naturally, many visitors stopped by to take a photo with the bust which acts like a guardian of the Arno River. Beyond the bridge, I saw many (probably unlicensed) peddlers of African descent selling belts, wallets and sunglasses on the streets. These people were probably immigrants from North African countries who had undertaken dangerous sea journeys to arrive at Italy, much like the early immigrants from China and India who settled in Singapore.

South of the River Arno, I strolled into the Boboli Gardens, a vast garden laid out in Renaissance style, complete with statues, lawns and ornate fountains. I particularly enjoyed the greenery and the crisp air in the garden and paused ever so often to admire the statues that adorned it. One statue made up of three marble figures especially caught my attention, and I immediately interpreted the story behind the sculptures in the form of a sonnet:[14]

---

[14]   The original sonnet was written in 40 minutes in the Boboli Gardens. I worked on it upon returning to Loughborough to fashion it into a sonnet, making it flow better and rhyme more naturally.

The Fallen Tale

'I saw three white figures in garden green,
Two big, one small, methought they set a scene:
Adam and Eve, and Sin, in Paradise,
Where Eve, deceived by Sin in shrewd disguise,
And spurred by Wisdom, God's Divine, had sunk
To depth so deep and steep as Wine made drunk,
Confessed in truth and pain, what new distress
Had found her out and plunged her down, suppressed
Her joy of Innocence, and Purity,
Which Adam could not give save Sympathy,
Himself a prey to Sin's bad fruit, but feel
The selfsame shame in nakedness revealed.
    So fair a pair on Earth was never shown,
    So sad a tale is always told and known.'

I spent another day in Florence with the intention of visiting the Uffizi Gallery and other art galleries. However, I decided against that for two important reasons: my funds were running low and my level of concentration was also depleting. Indeed, one needs a lot of energy to appreciate art pieces in museums. I did the next best thing: bought a copy of the guidebook to the Uffizi and brought it back to Loughborough so that I could enjoy the paintings in the Uffizi at my own leisure. I then wandered around town, bought some postcards to write to friends, and spent some time at Piazzale Michelangelo, an elevated park with a bronze replica of Michelangelo's statue of David. The panoramic view over the city from here was breath-taking and I was inspired to write a poem, entitled Paradise Restored, about my time with Daniela in Pisa two days ago. My creative juices flowed so naturally and liberally that I soon finished thirty lines.

I had thought of meeting Daniela again to bid her a final farewell. But I never met her again at the hostel after the first day. I wrestled within me and prayed if I should deliberately seek her out at the hostel or move on in my journey; I asked God for wisdom to make the right decision. Much as my flesh desired to spend more time with her, the spirit within me reminded me to seek wisdom and guidance from God.

It was with God's guidance that I chose Assisi as my next stop. So much peace and serenity had I in this town on a hill in central Italy that my creative juices flowed ever more profusely. In my first diary entry in Assisi, I recorded the following:

> 'God has been faithful in giving me the desires of my heart. To Assisi then He brought me, away from the loving yet unbearable tension of Florence. And what a sense of inner peace there was in the evening mass at Minerva Church. I was swept by the power of His holy presence, cleansed and mentally refreshed. And that gave me the mind to write to my Bible study leader and the Bookless family. Yes, certainly, Assisi is the best place for me. Up in the hills, amongst the holiest of priests and fathers, the atmosphere and the surrounding scenery have the effect of tranquilizing my restless soul and spirit, which can now settle down to prayerful prayers.'

Assisi was made famous by its patron saint, Saint Francis, whose biography is noteworthy. Born into a wealthy family, he squandered his youth on drinks and parties. However, later as a result of fighting in a war, he was imprisoned for nearly a year during which it was said that he received visions from God. Upon his release from prison, he responded to the voice of Christ to rebuild the Christian church and to live a life of poverty. He also had a special affinity with nature and animals and was subsequently made the patron saint of the environment and animals. Some of his words have a lasting influence on millions of followers across the world, such as "Lord, grant that I might not so much seek to be loved as to love" and "Where there is injury let me sow pardon".

As I walked up the slopes of this hill, I could attest to the simple lifestyle and the love of its people. There was so much music in the air; there was also much love. My soul rejoiced and celebrated as I captured the moments of ecstasy in my diary:

> 'This is most certainly a day to be alive, alive with the better and higher virtues of humanity. There is music in the air; there is also music in the hearts of the people. On the way to the Basilica of Saint Francis in Assisi, two souls render music to the passers-by: one with a violin, the other a flute. Such harmony they blend, such sweetness and melody their music effects, and floats, and drifts in this cool fresh air. Their performance seems to give them energy, revitalizing themselves as it refreshes others. Music, for the soul

within, has the embracing quality for the
souls without. And I once again have felt
the reverberating excitation of my heart,
to think on Wordsworth's humble and
rustic people,[15] and equate these two free
and joyous souls with them. I want to
write, to capture this momentary delight
of the heart and the mind, and to bring to
life months and years later this beautiful
memory of Assisi.'

At one point, the pen I was using refused to produce
any more ink. I shook it again and again, and that action
touched the hearts of a group of high school girls nearby.
One of them came up to offer me a pen. What a pleasant
surprise! I was visibly moved by their simple and kind
gesture and asked to take a photo of the five of them so as
to remember their goodness to me in the years to come.

That day, I visited the Basilica of Saint Francis, a
vast hillside Gothic church built in the 13th century. The
interior of the church was filled with frescoes completed
by numerous famous Italian artists, and the subject matter
ranged from stories found in the Old Testament and the
New Testament to the life of Saint Francis. They were a
visual feast to me as I spent many hours trying to figure
out the story behind each painting. In the evening, I
attended a mass called 'Blessings of the Holy Oils' at the
Cathedral of San Rufino and participated in the 'Way
of the Cross', a procession from the church to the streets
in some quarters. Though I was not a Catholic, I could

---

[15] William Wordsworth, an English poet, eulogized humble
and rustic people in many of his pastoral poems.

identify with the events leading up to the death and resurrection of Christ, which was the focus of that week leading up to Easter Sunday.

The final stop of my two-week journey was Rome, the capital city of Italy. Arising from my research prior to the trip, the must-see in this historic city for me were the Vatican City and its Sistine Chapel, the Spanish Steps, the Trevi Fountain and the Colosseum. I was intrigued by the fact that the Vatican City is regarded as an independent country despite the small land area it occupies within the city of Rome. The city-state has its own government, police, and issues its own stamps. On top of that, it is home to the largest church in the world, Saint Peter's Basilica, where the apostle Peter – one of the twelve disciples of Jesus -- was believed to be buried.

I paid my first visit to the Vatican City on a wet Good Friday morning on 1st April, 1988. Due to the overcast sky, St Peter's Basilica did not appear as spectacular as it looked on postcards and travel brochures. The interior, however, was not affected by the lack of sunshine that morning; it stood out as a masterpiece of art and architecture, an exquisite museum on its own. I saw people queuing for tickets for the Good Friday afternoon mass and collected one for myself. To be honest, it was not so much my desire to worship God but my wish for a religious experience in this famed cathedral that prompted me to join the mass. Pope John Paul II and his entourage of cardinals presided over the solemn service to commemorate the crucifixion of Christ. The entire proceeding did not appeal much to me as I was unschooled in both the languages used throughout the mass: Latin and Italian. Also, my energy level was waning as the day continued as I did not have a good night of rest at the railway station in Rome the night before.

My other consuming passion of visiting the Vatican City was to see the Sistine Chapel next to Saint Peter's Basilica. I wanted to be mesmerized by the paintings of Michelangelo on the walls and ceiling of the chapel. However, it was poor timing to do that on an Easter weekend: the long queue of visitors. Moreover, after spending another night at the railway station, I was not as sprightly as I normally would be. So as I did in Florence, I decided to buy a guidebook to enjoy the paintings of the Sistine Chapel at my leisure, and then found my way to the Spanish Steps, east of the River Tiber.

The Spanish Steps is an open area with steps shaped irregularly like the wings of a butterfly. It is a popular meeting place for young people, especially musicians and artists. I first learned about it when I read the biography of John Keats, an English Romantic poet who spent his last months in a house at the bottom of the Spanish Steps. When I arrived, the place was filled with people, sitting, standing, walking up and down the steps; it was as if the whole of Rome had gathered for a concert in that area. I lingered for a moment, soaked in the festive mood and then headed south to the nearby Trevi Fountain, one of the most famous fountains in the world. Here, I saw many people throwing coins into the fountain. It is believed that throwing one coin into the fountain will ensure one a return to Rome; two coins, find love; and three coins, wedding bells![16] I could not remember throwing any coin into the fountain as I was probably cynical about such superstition.

---

[16] Extracted from https://www.walksofitaly.com/blog/art-culture/9-surprising-facts-trevi-fountain-rome

The final monument I went to in Rome was the Colosseum, an oval amphitheater built in AD 72 using captured and enslaved Jews from Judea, and completed in AD 80. It was built for a capacity of 60, 000 or more spectators to enjoy gladiatorial fights and the hunting of wild animals. Later, however, it was also used as the execution ground for all sorts of criminals, including Roman army deserters, rebels, traitors, runaway slaves and those accused of anti-social behavior, such as Christians.[17] Regardless of the cruelty of such sports and events, the Colosseum is a fine example of robust architecture and engineering, considering the fact that it was built about 2,000 years ago and is still standing tall today.

When I was planning this trip, it did not occur to me that I would be spending the Holy Week weekend competing with visitors from other parts of the world for a bed in one of the many guesthouses in this city. As a result, I had to spend three consecutive nights at the railway station in Rome. To my surprise, sleeping at the station was not an unusual practice. All around the station, I saw many homeless people, probably penniless, making their beds out of a blanket or two, and using a piece of cardboard to lessen the cold of the concrete floor. In essence, I was putting into practice what I had learned: 'When in Rome, do as the Romans do!' In fact, by the third night, I was wise enough not to sleep in the waiting room (and risk being chased off by station masters in the unearthly hours of the morning) but occupied a corner in the open area where I could enjoy continuous sleep for many hours.

---

[17] Extracted from http://www.tribunesandtriumphs.org/ colosseum/roman-executions-at-the-colosseum.htm

On Easter Sunday, I woke up with renewed strength, having slept much better than the previous two nights. However, I did not desire to spend another night at the railway station; I longed for the comfort of a proper bed. Thus, I contacted the airline to change my flight at no extra cost to fly back to London a day earlier—on Easter Sunday itself. I thanked God there was a vacant seat on the flight that afternoon. At the airport in Rome, as I was waiting for the plane, I thanked God for all the people I met on this trip. Starting from Venice and ending in Rome, God had brought many lovely people across my path, and often in unexpected situations. These people had charmed my heart, and I felt that I had given a portion of myself to them, remembering them in my prayers. I also thanked God for enabling me to write prolifically on this journey; some of the pieces went into my creative writing portfolio, which were later submitted to my university professor for assessment.

I did not remember much of the flight from Rome to London. Most probably, I was too exhausted to take note of my surrounding. What I did recall was that I arrived back in Loughborough late in the night, as I had to take a three-hour National Express coach journey from London to Loughborough. As the accommodation in my hall of residence was booked only from the next day onward, I found myself knocking on the door of the Robertsons. Though my arrival was unannounced, they warmly welcomed me. It was an expression of love, unconditional love, at the most inconvenient time. Years later, I was to reflect on this incident and reminded myself to give to the needs of others, even if they come knocking on my door at an unearthly time.

L1 Lake Victoria
L2 Lake Tanganyika
L3 Lake Malawi
L4 Lake Kariba

KENYA

Kisumu

Nairobi

L1

Tarime

Mwanza

Waiamu Malindi

Mombasa

Tanga

Bagamoyo

Ujiji

L2

TANZANIA

INDIAN
OCEAN

Dar
es Salaam

MALAWI

Mbeya

Livingstonia

L3

Kapiri Mposhi

ZAMBIA

Lusaka
Kafue

Lilongwe

Mulanje
Mt.

Livingstone L4

Kariba

Monkey
Bay

MOZAMBIQUE

Victoria
Falls

HARARE

Bulawayo

ZIMBABWE

Map 5: Kenya, Tanzania, Zambia, Zimbabwe & Malawi

CHAPTER 6

Exploring the Heart of Darkness in Kenya and Tanzania

The heart is deceitful above all things and beyond cure. Who can understand it?

Jeremiah 17:9

Sometime in early 1988, I was glad to be informed by Operation Raleigh that I had been selected to participate in one of the many expeditions going to many different developing countries. As I scanned the list of dates and countries, Kenya seemed to be a probable option. However, before embarking on any expedition, one had to raise the amount required for the chosen destination. So, I spent the greater part of the first few months of 1988 writing to many companies in the United Kingdom, soliciting donation for my intended expedition to Kenya in the summer months. I must have sent out close to a hundred letters but received only a few replies. And out of those few replies, only one gave me a couple of hundred British pounds. While I was thankful for this singular positive response, it was far from the amount I needed to raise. So when the deadline for confirmation of participation came, I had to sadly forgo the opportunity due to a lack of financial support.

The difficulty in raising funds for the Operation Raleigh trip to Kenya did not detract me from enjoying my studies in both English and Physical Education as there were many options to choose from in the second year. For instance, for English, I took up the challenge to enroll in Creative Writing and Canadian Literature, both of which I had interest in but not much knowledge about; for Physical Education, I chose a module on Sports and Society, in which I learned much about the culture, politics and economics behind international competitions in sports. I also rejoiced in the fact that at the age of twenty two, having had absolutely no prior training in gymnastics, I could perform some skills such as the front and back hip circles on the horizontal bar with sufficient poise and body tension. This was achieved based on my knowledge of the principles of rotation in Biomechanics and a willingness to execute it: putting theory into application. I was passionate about my studies and learning.

After my examinations in late June, I was still undecided about what to do for the summer months but I had made up my mind not to go home to Singapore. Just then, I read a note from the university YHA (Youth Hostel Association) Club notice board inviting interested students to sign up for a five-day trip to Scotland. Having heard much about the rugged mountains of Scotland, I wasted no time in signing up for the trip. I was not disappointed. The natural beauty of Scotland comprising its mountains (called 'bens') and lakes (called 'lochs') awed me. Surprisingly, the weather in southern Scotland then was even warmer than in Loughborough, so much so that we were able to go trekking around Loch Lomond and climb Ben Lomond in shorts. However, the same cannot be said of the water in Loch Lomond. It was icy cold despite the warm ground temperature. I tried swimming in it but after a short period of time, I had to abandon the activity as I was shivering uncontrollably. Still, the vastness and rugged beauty of Scotland captivated me; given another opportunity, I would like to see Scotland again.

Soon after returning to Loughborough from Scotland, I was informed that I had performed well in my second academic year with an overall grade of Second Upper class. Truly, I thanked God for the results. My weekly commitment to study the Bible and to attend Sunday morning church service had not caused my academic pursuit to suffer; instead, I had become more efficient and productive in the use of time as a result of additional commitments. One verse from the Bible was to be my focal point and anchor as I persevered through the weeks and months of churning out assignments: 'Give thanks in all circumstances, for this is God's will for you in Christ Jesus.' (1 Thessalonians 5:18). Upon this verse I meditated much and resolved to give thanks whatever the results of my academic studies. I wrote a postcard to my sister informing her of my results and mentioned that I had not confirmed my plans for the summer months.

However, in the space of a week after my return from Scotland, I made up my mind to spend the summer months in Africa. The foremost reason was that I had, months earlier, intended to spend the entire summer in Kenya through my participation in Operation Raleigh. Now that the plan would not be realized, I could still visit the country on my own shoestring budget; more than that, I could also venture beyond the borders of Kenya to see other African countries. At the back of my mind, I concluded that African countries would be a lot more inexpensive compared to European countries, and in the event that my finances could not last me the entire two and a half months in Africa, I was willing to seek some temporary employment, like what I did in Israel the year before. And so armed with a copy of *Africa on a Shoestring*, published by Lonely Planet, and zest for adventure, I embarked on an extraordinary journey to Africa.

I had a rude introduction to Kenya. Arriving at Jomo Kenyatta International Airport in Nairobi, Kenya close to midnight on 9 July 1988, I had no other transport options except to hire a taxi to fetch me into the city center, some 18 kilometers away. The 20-minute journey cost me a massive sum of 250 Kenyan shilling,[18] which was very expensive by local standards. Along the way, I could not see much of the landscape of this city; it was pitch darkness most of the way till we entered the city center. The next morning, along Kenyatta Avenue, I saw two Kenyan flags and a banner stretched across the entrance to State House Road, with these words on it: 'Kenyans wish our Excellency long life and continued good health'. I wondered if the banner was put up by the common people or some government officials who were bent on

---

[18] Back in 1988, 1 British pound was equivalent to 30 Kenyan shilling. Looking back, I must have been fleeced by the taxi driver.

courting the favour of the then ruling President, Daniel Arap Moi.[19] At that time, I was not sufficiently informed of Kenyan politics and culture to be able to answer this question.

In Nairobi, I was to find both worshippers of God and worshippers of Mammon in the next few days. On Sunday, I visited Nairobi Pentecostal Church along Valley Road. It was a new experience for me to worship in a predominantly African church. Back in Loughborough, even though there were Africans amongst the congregation, they were few in terms of numbers; here, they were the majority and numbered in hundreds, and their strong voices came together powerfully as they worshipped God. From the church weekly bulletin given to me, I noted that there would be three services that Sunday. Also, the church had a strong emphasis on prayer: there would be daily prayers from 6.00 to 7.30 a.m. and 1 to 2 p.m. from Monday to Friday; each Tuesday at 6 p.m. there would be a weekly prayer; and in two weeks' time, there would be a 'whole night prayer'. At the back of the bulletin, a list of names of members under 'full membership', 'associate membership' and 'junior membership' was published; the list identified the people as belonging to the church, giving them a sense of belonging to the body of Christ.

In contrast to the church, I also witnessed the ugly manifestation of greed for Mammon in Nairobi. On the second morning in that city, I was accosted by a young man in a public area who 'desperately' needed help. He claimed to be a student from South Africa and due to some emergency needed to go home, but he lacked funds for

---

[19] The answer to this question became obvious when years later, investigations into his Presidency were made.

the homeward journey. He furnished me with so many details in response to my many questions and sounded so convincing that I believed him then and donated 200 Kenyan shilling to ease his predicament. My heart brimmed with joy for having helped a desperate soul, but my joy was short-lived. Soon after that episode, I was approached by another person who needed financial help for another kind of emergency. It dawned upon me then that there were many crooks in this city who specialized in fabricating stories and fleecing unsuspecting foreigners of their money.[20] Personally, this was an invaluable introductory lesson into travelling in Africa for me.

My introduction to Africa also included visits to Kenya National Archives and Nairobi National Museum, both of which were educational. In the former, I learned about the political history of Kenya through the photographs and documents on display, and the cultures of its tribal peoples through the wood and metal carvings. In the latter, there was a rich collection of specimens on the wildlife of Kenya—birds, animals and fish, and the tribal crafts used to hunt them. I was thrilled to see such a large collection of wildlife and secretly wished that I might see some of the animals in a wildlife reserve, alive and breathing, if I still had enough money at the end of my journey. Thus far, the few days in Nairobi had caused me to part with a disproportionate amount of the money meant for the entire two and a half months. I would probably need to work at some point during this long journey.

---

[20]   Online sources bear testimony to the many different scams experienced by tourists in Kenya, such as this site: https://travelscams.org/africa/kenya/

When I flew into Nairobi, I had no sense of what I would do, what route of advance I would take, and above all, what God wanted me to do in Africa. However, by the fourth day, I had decided to move westward toward Lake Victoria and from there travel southward to Tanzania. It was with this intention that I found myself travelling on an 8-hour bus journey from Nairobi to Kisumu, arriving in the late afternoon. Along the way, the bus skirted round the northern edge of Lake Nakuru, famed for its flamingoes, passed through many towns and villages with their schools and churches of all kinds of denominations and names, before finally pulling into the third largest city of Kenya, Kisumu. After spending so many hours in the bus, I was glad to disembark and exercise my legs.

Kisumu struck me as a rather small and sleepy city. The city center seemed to be clustered around the Kisumu Bus Park; the Kisumu Municipal Market, selling fruits, vegetables and spices; and the Municipal Fish Market, selling fish species from Lake Victoria like the Nile perch and Tilapia. I met three young college students, Joseph, Kenn and Jeremiah, near the bus park and they were keen to befriend me, a non-African all by myself. They showed me around the city center and then treated me to my first 'ugali' (a type of maize flour porridge made in Africa) meal, eaten together with some vegetable stew. It is somewhat like the Chinese steamed bun or 'mantou' except that ugali is made of cornmeal flour. I appreciated their hospitality and ate the simple meal heartily.

The next morning, Joseph and Kenn offered to be my guides around Kisumu. To be honest, I did not find the city interesting and lively; it was made up of the usual shops, banks, schools, and places of religious worship. However, I did find the way the locals made use of the lake both ingenious and uneducated. I saw people driving their vehicles into the shallow water of the lake and washing their cars there. In the process, they must have polluted the water with whatever fuels used to power the engines. They were unschooled in the knowledge of such pollution, even though they had been consuming fish that came from the lake itself. This scene made me appreciate the public education that is found in many developed countries.

By the lake, I also witnessed a frenzy in construction of houses. Plots of land were fenced up and many laborers busied themselves with laying the foundations of the buildings. It was a sign of economic development; it could also be a sign of the widening income gap of the people in this country, where the rich raced ahead of the common people and occupied the prime lands in the city, typically those which offer a lake view. With nothing much to hold me back in Kisumu, I decided to leave for Tanzania the next day.

Crossing the Kenya-Tanzania border was an interesting and eye-opening experience. While travelling in a matutu (a privately-owned minibus) enroute to Magori, a Kenyan town near the border, I bought a bunch of bananas and offered some to the bus passengers around me. After eating, I saw them throw the banana skins out of the windows. Coming from Singapore where littering was and still is strictly forbidden, I was aghast at their lack of civic-mindedness in maintaining cleanliness in public areas. However, soon after that I saw cows moving towards the banana skins and eating them up. How interesting! Nothing goes to waste! On the other hand, I witnessed the greed of the driver and the bus conductor in picking up more passengers than was legally allowed.

The driver had to outwit the traffic police stationed at various checkpoints. For instance, before arriving at a designated checkpoint, all standing passengers were asked to get down and walk across the checkpoint and be picked up by the same matutu after the checkpoint, or wait for another relatively empty matutu. It was also an eye-opener to see how some of the passengers argue with the bus conductor concerning the fares they had to pay.

At Migori, I had no intention to stay for a night and thus hopped onto another matutu bound for the border at Isebania. After clearing the Isebania Kenya Immigration Office, there was a stretch of no-man's land, about half a kilometer long, filled with various kinds of shops, roadside peddlers and black-market moneychangers. I walked across this stretch all the way to the Tanzania Immigration Office at Sirari, where my passport was stamped, allowing me to remain in the country for two weeks. At the next bus stand some 500 meters away, I hopped unto another matutu and soon arrived at Tarime, a town 20 kilometers further south. Not wanting to arrive after last light at Mwanza, my intended destination for the day, I decided to spend the night at Tarime.

Tarime had a certain laid-back charm to it. In this small town I was to meet Asseno, the owner of a technical equipment and hardware store. He was probably in his late twenties and spoke reasonably good English. As I was clearly a non-African (or perhaps considered a white man by some), many young curious children crowded around me, their eyes never seemed to be taken away from me. I gestured to them that I would take a photo of them in front of Asseno's shop and they gamely posed for me: five boys standing behind and two little girls seated on the steps in front, their bodies veered outward, forming a 'V' in between them. In no time, I found a good friend in Asseno and he was keen to help me get a teaching position in a school in Tarime.

The next morning, the town brightened to a certain consciousness. People were seen roaming about engaging in one activity or another. Some women and girls balanced baskets of goods or fruits on their heads, heading in various directions. I walked with Asseno to a secondary school with the hope of securing a temporary teaching job. The school principal, likely one of his good friends, was friendly enough to spare us his time. After some exchange between him and Asseno in Swahili language, I was told that it was not the right timing as the school was having its summer vacation till mid-August. As I had no intention to remain in Tarime till then, I took it as a closed door from God and decided to move on to Mwanza, a bigger city on the southern shore of Lake Victoria.

The journey to Musoma and onward to Mwanza was painfully slow and treacherous. The old bus, heavily laden with passengers and goods, broke down three times in the space of four hours, prolonging the entire journey by hours. On top of that, the journey was made rough by the uneven road surfaces and occasional potholes. But the scenery along the way was superb. Endless stretches of wild and untamed plains were decorated in a random fashion by huts, gigantic rocks and herds of cattle that grazed the fields. Occasionally, a predatory bird would glide across the sky, surveying the ground for its prey. Around me, I did not detect any anger or frustration on the faces of the passengers; to them, this must be an ordinary affair that was very much part of life. That evening, upon my arrival at Mwanza, I wrote to some friends to share with them my African journey up to that point, and mentioned with no uncertain hope that "out of Africa will emerge a Singaporean, a youth who will have a fair degree of understanding and appreciation of African life and culture." Indeed, the journey had taught me one important lesson: have patience when travelling in Africa.

Much like Kisumu in Kenya, Mwanza is a port city on the shore of Lake Victoria in Tanzania. There was not much of interest to me here except the Bismarck Rock, a precariously balanced boulder atop a group of rock outcrops in the lake next to the Kamanga ferry pier. Here, one could sit for hours watching young children bathing in the lake, fishermen washing the haul of fish from their catch, ferries arriving and departing from the nearby ferry terminal, and cows grazing nonchalantly on the grass next to the lake.

To keep myself occupied, I bought two books: *I Love Idi Amin* by Bishop Festo Kivengere, and *Man and Development* by Julius Nyerere, the founding President of Tanzania. I read with interest the story of triumph in the midst of suffering and persecution in Uganda under the former dictator Idi Amin, and also learned something about the philosophy behind the development of Tanzania in the first twenty years. How much of the content of my reading I understood I was unable to ascertain, but without doubt I had gained some knowledge of East African history and appreciated the difficulties in uniting and developing a nation that was largely divided by more than a hundred tribal languages, with most of its people illiterate.

The widespread illiteracy and its consequent poverty in many African countries made social and infrastructural development difficult to accomplish. Being in Tanzania and witnessing the sad state of its development despite its independence from British colonial masters since the early 1960s (more than 20 years ago), there was a longing for me to help the country. Perhaps it was in this frame of mind that I met Laurent Munyu, a 27-year-old born-again Christian. Through our conversation, I learnt that he was raising funds for his wedding, scheduled for the end of the month. He seemed to me a sincere and genuine person, and the spirit within me prompted me to bless him with a gift of 2000 Tanzanian shilling (about 12 British pounds). To me, I was helping a fellow Christian in a less developed country progress and develop in his life. Shortly after that, I was successful in buying a bus ticket from Mwanza to Dar-es-Salaam, a journey that would take two days traversing the country from the north-west to the east coast. It was such a relief that I did not have to wait a few days to procure a ticket.

The long bus journey to Dar-es-Salaam was fraught with delay and danger. The bus was originally scheduled to depart from the bus park at 9 a.m. but it did not show up. For umpteen times, I had asked various individuals about its arrival time and the usual reply was 'soon' or 'it is coming'. Though they could not tell me specifically when the bus would arrive, they had the unyielding faith that it would appear. After hearing such standard replies repeatedly, I gathered that 'time' was not regarded as a fixed and precise concept but a relative one in the country. Rather than being specific about time, like "the bus will arrive at 9 a.m.", the locals tend to believe that "the bus will come soon" without defining the word 'soon'.

Eventually, the bus arrived and, after all passengers had loaded their bags and baskets, left at 3.45 p.m. But after less than two hours, it broke down for the first time, and then continued to break down no less than four more times for the entire journey. However, the locals did not seem to mind; the intermittent breakdowns served the purpose of allowing them to periodically walk about, stretch their legs and relieve themselves behind some bushes. As for me, I made use of the opportunities to write occasional letters to my family and friends, sharing with them my journey and venting at times my frustration arising from the numerous delays.

To compound the matter, the bus driver overloaded the bus with illegal standing passengers. When the bus was climbing a steep slope, the standing passengers as well as some of the seated ones would be asked to get down the bus and walk up the slope; likewise, when it was negotiating down a steep slope, passengers also had to disembark for fear that the brakes would not work efficiently. My initial response to this phenomenon was to accuse the driver of being unscrupulous, endangering the lives of passengers by overloading the bus. However, on second thought, given the irregular public transport services for long journeys in this country, it was little wonder why the passengers did not mind the hassle and the potential danger. They were only too glad to be able to ride on some form of transportation and get to their destinations, albeit slowly.

Eternity in the form of forty hours passed me by as the bus finally arrived at Dar-es-Salaam. It was literally light at the end of a long journey as the bus made its way into the city at the break of a new day. I was exhausted by the journey, having been jolted from my seat at the back of a long bus every time the vehicle ran over a pothole – and there were hundreds of them along the way, a sign of poor road maintenance as a result of insufficient government funds. I was also starving, having survived on snacks and fruits for the past two days. To satisfy my basic needs for food and rest, I checked into a budget hotel which happened to run a bar on its ground floor. It was a grave mistake, one which I would not forget.

The oppressive heat of the day propelled me to buy a bottle of beer at the bar in the evening. I had no intention to linger and socialize with other patrons. However, before I had finished drinking my bottle of beer, a few senior civil servants drinking ceaselessly not far from me offered to buy me another drink. They appeared tipsy and I did not wish to insult them by rejecting the drink. So I sat there longer than I had wanted to, drinking and smiling at them, but not communicating much with them verbally. At the earliest convenient moment, when I had finished the bottle of beer, I excused myself from them, citing tiredness as a reason. Back in my room, I chided myself for stepping into the bar and putting myself in possible danger of over-drinking. I prayed and retired to bed.

But such restless sleep had I that first night in Dar-es-Salaam. The mosquitoes in my room were mercilessly assaulting me and waking me from my drowsiness. I woke up about two hours later to find swollen spots on my face and bare arms; my body was perspiring profusely due to the heat and stuffiness of the room. The almost brand-new fan hung motionless from the ceiling—not working! To add to my annoyance, the loud music from the disco lounge below invaded the privacy of my room. Then as I walked past two fashionably dressed girls on the way to the toilet, one of them made a pass at me. They were prostitutes, probably. I was immediately reminded of the pervasive existence of AIDS in some African countries and promptly ignored the girls. To a new arrival like me, this city was a breeding ground for mosquitoes, prostitutes, heavy drinkers and profiteers.

My impressions of Dar-es-Salaam were also contributed by a half-naked man I came across at the beach. A solitary figure who called the make-shift shelter composed of a few pieces of wood his home, he volunteered in comprehensible English a running commentary on the incompetence of the government in Tanzania. Independence according to him did not result in people living a better life; on the contrary, the conditions of the country and its economy had worsened since then. The government did not educate the people on the various means to cultivate and manage the resources of the land, and many were driven by economic circumstances into unemployment while some survived by peddling small quantities of food and drinks. Still, many others who lost jobs ended up idling away their life, sitting around the city and doing nothing constructive. The quality of education had also deteriorated since independence. More children were leaving school after their primary school education. Consequently, juvenile delinquency rates increased tremendously. Meanwhile, the rich continued to thrive and establish themselves in high ministerial posts. To him, the whole logic and rationale behind independence was ill-conceived and a sham.

The monologue by the man on the beach stirred me to ask questions pertaining to political and economic independence. What good is it to be given freedom (in independence) if one cannot handle the responsibilities (of self-governance) that come with it? What good would independence bring to the people if they subsequently have no jobs and income? On the other hand, there is always an argument for human pride and dignity in any struggle for independence, and such sentiments are often considered far more important than economic gain or stability. Furthermore, were the colonial masters not exploiting the natives and the resources of Africa when they were in power here? My mind was in a flux. I had no ready answers for such questions. To me, having witnessed the miracles that a clean and capable government under the leadership of Lee Kuan Yew had effected in Singapore, the more important question was not about who the rulers were, but what values they stood for; an honest and sincere government, regardless of its skin color – white or black, can bring about social and economic development for its people. To achieve that, the forces of corruption arising from greed must be minimized and controlled, if not eliminated.

One potent form of human corruption in Africa was slave trade. My visit to Bagamoyo, a coastal town some 60 kilometers north of Dar-es-Salaam, gave me a glimpse into the history of slavery in this country. Fronted by a stretch of beautiful beach lined with coconut trees, Bagamoyo marked the end of a long trek for slaves originating from Central Africa. From Ujiji on the shore of Lake Tanganyika, the slave traders' caravan route went over 1200 kilometers and ended in Bagamoyo,[21] where slaves would be shipped to Zanzibar, an island opposite Bagamoyo, and subsequently sold by the Arabic traders and transported to India, Arabic countries, Persia and other parts of Africa.

Fortunately, some of the slaves were ransomed by the Roman Catholic Mission (from 1870 to 1920) in Zanzibar,

---

[21] Extracted from 'The Central Slave and Ivory Trade Route' found in https://whc.unesco.org/en/tentativelists/2095/

and later also in Bagamoyo, before they were sent to the slave markets in Zanzibar. The newly ransomed slaves were taught some African trades and their children given elementary education by the Catholic missionaries.[22] In Bagamoyo, I also came across the name of 'Dr David Livingstone', a Scottish Protestant missionary and physician who was very much a slave abolitionist. His courage and determination in navigating the hazardous terrain of Africa in the mid-19th century really impressed me. Such missionaries were truly emissaries of light in a continent filled with darkness, corruption, and greed. Their efforts contributed to the end of slave trade in East Africa in 1922.

Many years ago, when I was a junior college student, I studied a novella, *Heart of Darkness*, written in 1899 by a Polish-English novelist, Joseph Conrad. The narrator of the story, Marlow, tells a story of his journey up the Congo River to meet a successful but ailing ivory trader, Kurtz. Their meeting and conversation, and their subsequent journey down the Congo River, convince Marlow that deep in the heart of Africa lies a 'civilized' man whose heart is as dark and depraved as the 'savages' of the continent: a man's heart, and not so much his physical surrounding (Africa) is really where cruelty and wanton violence lie. As I recalled this story and the people I had encountered thus far on my journey in Africa—cheats, slave traders, prostitutes, I could not but agree with Conrad about the depravity of man's heart; but I

---

[22]   Cited from '*A Study of the East African Slave Trade in Bagamoyo*' retrieved from https://digitalcollections.sit. edu/cgi/viewcontent.cgi?referer=https://www.google. com/&httpsredir=1&article=1942&context=isp_collection

had also learned of the valiant efforts of missionaries to oppose human oppression and slavery. I reminded myself to be objective when describing this continent: amidst the darkness, there was also light, no matter how dim and insignificant it appeared.

CHAPTER 7

Being Up Close and Personal with Zambians and Zimbabweans

He lifted me out of the slimy pit, out of the mud and mire; he set my feet on a rock and gave me a firm place to stand.

Psalm 40:2

After more than two weeks in Kenya and Tanzania, I was ready to venture further south into Zambia. From the Lonely Planet guidebook, I learned that the government of China, in its zeal to win diplomatic support in Africa in the late 1960s, had agreed to help build a railway line running from the port city of Dar-es-Salaam in east Tanzania to Kapiri Mposhi in central Zambia. This line is called Tazara, an acronym for Tanzania-Zambia Railway, and it was completed in 1976. The primary purpose was to help transport goods from Zambia's Copperbelt to the coast for export without relying on

Rhodesia (later known as Zimbabwe) and South Africa, both of which were ruled by the capitalist whites then.

From the guidebook, I also gathered that as a student, I was entitled to apply for a 50% discount in train tickets. Seizing the opportunity to save some money, I went through the hassle of filling up some forms and bought a one-way second-class ticket which cost me only 935 Tanzanian shilling (equivalent to 5.5 British pound). I was ready to sit back and enjoy the scenery on this 40-hour train journey, travelling from Dar es Salaam in Tanzania to Kapiri Mposhi in Zambia.

The congested Dar-es-Salaam soon gave way to wide open plains with rolling hills in the background. The train passed through small towns, rural villages and even the northern edge of Selous Game Reserve. In the distance, one could at times catch sight of some wildlife such as zebras, elephants and antelopes moving among the bushes as the sun set over the entire plains. In some villages, smoke was rising out of the chimneys of some mud huts topped with straws and brick houses covered with zinc-sheets, suggesting domestic activities such as the preparation of the evening meal. The entire landscape gradually darkened like the shutter of a camera shutting down, permitting little or no light to pass through it. But the train continued to plough on in the darkness, cutting through more towns and villages along the way, and producing a regular and rhythmic droning sound as its wheels continued to rub against the railway track.

The next day, the train crossed over many bridges and rivers as it headed towards the Zambian border. Occasionally, it rolled on tracks hung high above the river and then went through tunnels bore through mountains, giving one a panoramic view of the surrounding mountain ranges at one moment and pitch darkness the next. But mostly, the train traversed through the backyards of small towns and villages, dotted with clusters of banana and coconut trees, where villagers could be seen labouring on their farmlands or herding their cattle in a routine, unhurried manner.

At bigger stations such as Mbeya, the scene was more animated. African women and children draped in colorful outfits could be seen balancing plastic pails and basins on their heads as they moved towards the approaching train, ready to sell their produce to passengers on board the train. They offered fruits and vegetables such as tomatoes, pumpkins, sweet potatoes, coconuts, bananas and more, eager to make some money from their trade. Some small boys, however, simply gestured to the passengers in the carriages with their fingers, begging for money to buy some food.

The train finally pulled into Kapiri Mposhi in central Zambia in the wee hours of the morning after almost 40 hours. With no intention to remain there, I quickly bought an onward ticket to Lusaka, the capital city, where I stopped over for two days. There was nothing particularly interesting about this city. Like the rest of the country, Lusaka was still recovering from decades of political and military support for liberation from white rule in other southern African countries; such efforts had almost bankrupted its economy. It was only after I had travelled some 60 km further south from Lusaka to a small town called Kafue that I found something arresting; there, I witnessed a slaughter scene and composed a poem:

A Slaughter Scene

His leg was tied to a tree trunk nearby,
His movement restricted,
He could stand or choose to sit,
But wait he must,
Helpless and hopeless,
Upon such hour to be led
To the slaughter ground.

He was much superior in strength,
He resisted their combined force,
But being an animal,
He had no such craft
To counter their method,
To free himself
Of his final fate.

Soon both his hind legs were tied,
His body was struck,
He could not turn right or left,
Surrounded on both sides
By men with sticks,
He was ushered forcibly
To meet their wants.

With great might he was felled,
His tail was used
As an agent against him,
His single hind legs
Betrayed his resistance,
He struggled in vain
As his moment neared.

Now all his legs were bound,
He lay still
Like a carcass,
Knowing his hour had come at last,
Waiting to be dragged
To sharp blades and heads
On high slaughter ground.

They found his head the most
Stubborn and useless,
But of his four legs,
They were still worth
Some weakening kwachas,
To buy new axes and knives
For younger cows and bulls.

This slaughter scene took place at a common cattle market to which nearby villagers brought their cattle and where wealthy consumers congregated to bid for a good buy. I was fortunate to be given permission to photograph the entire long drawn-out process of felling a bull, which required four or five persons pulling it from different directions; immobilizing it while it lay on the ground; dragging it onto a platform; and finally slaughtering it with sharp axes and knives. It was a gruesome act of men overpowering a beast. Interestingly, most of the people gathered there were men; there was no display of emotions as this was a common scene on a market day in that town. However, to me, the process was most painful (to watch) and primitive, so much so that it stirred me to pen a poem.

Apart from writing my diary and an occasional poem, I also used any spare time I had on my journey to write to family and friends back in Singapore and England. Just as

I was about to finish writing a letter to the Crowhursts, a young man in his twenties who spoke fairly good English approached me and offered to show me his father's farm some distance away, with the option to stay there for a few days. Wanting to experience life on an African farm, I followed him without much hesitation and climbed into the front seat of a big white truck, on which was printed the name 'Kalinda', his family name. He introduced himself as 'Cliff' and informed me that the farm was in Nega Nega, a short distance away by truck.

Weaving through some narrow lanes for half an hour or more, the truck finally arrived at a big farm in the middle of nowhere. As far as my eyes could travel, I did not see any other farm within half a kilometre. The surrounding was sparsely vegetated with lonesome trees here and there; there was a pervasive brownness and dryness to the entire landscape. As the truck came to a halt, a few young men suddenly appeared, all ready to load the fully filled gunny sacks onto the back of the truck. It was a labor-intensive and back-breaking task but they did it with so much glee. After they had completed the task, I took a photo of them posing in front of the truck, each of them wearing a smile that seemed to convey their sense of pride in their work. Their figures cast long shadows on the ground as the sun set slowly but surely on this big farm.

The next morning, I awoke to the chill typical of the early hours when the sun had just begun to rise in the east. The surrounding was already visible, but the white moon still hung so casually in the sky. I visited the latrine (there was no flushing toilet here) and then went to join a few others who had already gathered round a fire to warm themselves. One of the men stood up to offer me the best wooden stool but I declined, not wanting to be treated as a VIP. Not far from us, two sheets were spread on the ground, with some garments folded in small bundles like improvised pillows. I cast my curious eyes on them, and soon one of the men explained that two of them had been spending the night there to guard the harvested corn from wild animals. Presumably, they were the hired hands on this farm and had to spend the night doing sentry duties. Soon, the eldest son of the Kalinda family appeared. After an exchange of pleasantries, he uttered a few words to the others, and everybody left the little fire and went about the day's work.

I was given a brief introduction to the farm. On this farm, a big community was built around the senior Kalinda who married a few wives. Naturally, there were many children and grandchildren. Some lived in the single-storey white house with many rooms, while others in separate small units made of bricks and mud, topped with zinc sheets. Interspersed among these buildings were a few mud huts with conical roofs made of straw—these were the family kitchens, I was informed. Not too far from these buildings and huts was a fenced-up open area approximately the size of a boxing ring in which was stored the harvested corns with their husks removed. Next to this ring stood a machine, which could separate the kernels from the cobs. Tugged away in a corner of the farm was a mill where women could grind their sacks of corn into powder. At another corner of the farm, there was a huge enclosed area about half the size of a football field where farm cattle were kept.

I was amazed by the great teamwork and harmony that existed within the Kalinda family. There was no sign of jealousy or enmity (or at least I did not see or sense any) amongst the different wives and amongst the children of different mothers. Everybody seemed to belong to the big family and contributed heartily to its agricultural output. Women were seen feeding the dry corns into the machine and at the other end of the machine filling the empty gunny sacks with the kernels; men were mainly in charge of weighing, recording and stockpiling the sacks of corn for export; small boys were given the task to hand-milk the cows while little girls helped take care of their younger siblings or helped their mothers prepare meals in the mud huts. Meanwhile, the senior Kalinda, who commanded a mixture of respect and fear from the youngest to the oldest in the family, walked his rounds, inspecting and supervising the work with patience and a keen eye. For the week I spent there, I was the resident photographer capturing the joy of the people on this farm. What a pity it was that I could not interview them as most of them did not speak much English and I knew nothing of their language, Bemba.

Language barrier was not the only reason for my lack of verbal communication with most people on the farm. I was also physically sapped of energy after three weeks on the road with minimal food and water on some days. I felt all the frailness within me, as though I had just gone through a weary battle. In addition, the heat from mid-morning till late afternoon was unbearably intense for me, and there was no fan in my room. All I wanted to do was to be left alone, to lie in bed and to speak to my Father, God. I poured out my feelings to Him and asked Him for divine healing. In this one week on the farm, I read my Bible voraciously, covering books like Ruth, Daniel and Esther among others.

God did hear my prayer for strength. On one of the days, I felt strong enough to join some members of the

Kalinda family on a shopping trip to Mazabuka, a biggish town one and a half hours away from Nega Nega. What made the trip interesting was not the scenery along the way, nor the beauty of Mazabuka, but that the Kalinda family's truck operated like a bus, picking up passengers enroute every now and then. There was no public transport along this route, and villagers usually walked from one village to another, or hitched a ride from passing vehicles. On the way back to Nega Nega, the truck was literally sardine-packed, and most of the passengers - both male and female - were standing instead of seated. Thus, the truck travelled rather slowly. I was impressed by the generosity of the Kalinda family in providing transportation for the common people!

It was easy to lose track of time and days on this farm. I did not see anybody wearing a watch, nor was there a clock on the wall in my room. Here, their concept of time was not measured in terms of hours but by the rhythm of the rising and setting of the sun. They instinctively knew what to do according to the position of the sun; their activities moved in tandem with the lengths of the shadows cast on the ground. When the sky brightened each morning, they went about preparing breakfast; when it darkened at the end of the day, they again retreated to their kitchens to prepare dinner. In between, they worked and rested. Their lives were intricately connected with and dependent on nature: They worked the land and it yielded food for them; their activities flowed according to the season of planting and harvesting, from which they noted the passage of time.

I was thankful for the privilege of being part of this community for a week. As a guest and an unofficial resident photographer, I was given a glimpse of the daily life of these people on the farm during harvest time. I marveled at their dedication to work, evidenced by the huge stockpile of grains of corn, and the lack of domestic squabbles amongst them. The children had very little in terms of material goods; in fact, they did not wear any shoes or slippers but went about barefooted. Despite this apparent lack, they were cheerful and smiled very spontaneously whenever I took photos of them. During my sojourn there, I did not witness any child throwing a tantrum, demanding something from his or her parents. Instead those who were old enough helped with the chores on the farm, while those who were too young were looked after by their older siblings. Their natural contentment was a stark contrast to some of the spoiled brats found in more developed countries.

The week on Kalinda farm had afforded me a good rest. Before I left the farm, Cliff handed me a letter written in English. He expressed his interest for us to keep writing to each other and apologized for serving me 'one type of food every lunch, dinner and breakfast'— corn porridge. In return, I promised to send him the photos taken on the farm and thanked him for his and his family's hospitality. To me, apart from the rest, it had been educational to experience life on an African farm, an experience that probably money could not buy. My only regret was my inability to communicate with most of them in the language that they used. Still I thanked God for the memories.

I continued my journey southward by train to Livingstone, a Zambian town near the border with Zimbabwe and named after the Scottish explorer and missionary. Onboard the train, I met a Japanese lady who was heading for Livingstone as well. She was working as an overseas volunteer based in Lusaka. The entire train journey took about 15 hours and we arrived at Livingstone railway station in the unearthly hour of one hour past midnight. Not wishing to roam the town at this hour, we decided to spend the night in our sleeping bags at the railway station. It was something I had done before a few months back in Italy. The only difference to me was that Livingstone is a smaller and quieter place compared to Venice or Rome and therefore should be safer. So we unrolled our sleeping mats and sleeping bags and slipped into them, under the curious and watchful eyes of a few Africans standing nearby.

My time in Livingstone was short but meaningful. I visited the Livingstone Museum where I learned more about the life and achievements of Doctor Livingstone, tools and weapons used in African tribal warfare, as well as the rituals and witchcraft commonly practised amongst the people. On 9th August 1988, Singapore's 23rd birthday, I wrote to my sister in Singapore, telling her that I was proud of my country and its immense progress since independence in 1965, especially after having seen the state of development in Kenya, Tanzania and Zambia. All the three countries gained independence from the United Kingdom a year or more before Singapore but the development in Singapore was truly far more advanced than these countries in East Africa.

The land crossing from Zambia into Zimbabwe at Victoria Falls was the most spectacular in terms of scenery. After a short bus ride of about ten kilometres from Livingstone to the Zambia Department of Immigration – Victoria Falls Border Post, I proceeded to cross the border by foot. The Zambian and Zimbabwean immigration posts were separated by a distance of two kilometres, including a 200-metre long metal bridge spanning across the mighty Zambezi River. Along this stretch of road, many visitors sauntered and marveled at the amazing falls and the huge rainbow overhanging the falls. Unfortunately, I was unable to bask in the beauty of the scenery for long as the intensity of the sun effected a headache in me which bothered me with every step that I took. I was glad that the immigration customs at both ends were trouble-free; my only regret then was that I did not have much time to gaze at the unsurpassed beauty of the falls from the Zimbabwean side. I had to hurry to the railway station at Victoria Falls, Zimbabwe.

My first impression of Zimbabwe was that the facilities and infrastructures were better maintained than those in Kenya, Tanzania and Zambia. This, in my opinion, was due to the fact that Zimbabwe gained independence from the British only as recently as 1980. At Victoria Falls train station, I was surprised that I could purchase my train ticket using Traveller's Cheques (TC) in British pounds. In all other previous countries, I had to change TC into local currencies in an official bank before making any purchase. The convenience at the train station meant that I could purchase a ticket on time to travel on the night train to Bulawayo, departing at 7 p.m., and also have some Zimbabwean dollars to begin my journey in this country. I really thanked God for it.

I arrived at Bulawayo the next morning a washed-out wanderer. Not responding to my bodily signals of frailty, I took a day trip to Tshabalala Game Sanctuary, situated about 10 km south of the city center. It turned out to be a complete waste of time, a great disappointment! I did not see any interesting species such as giraffe, kudu, zebra, impala and wildebeest as mentioned in the guidebook.

The day trip was the last straw as my body broke down completely the day after; I was physically in a pathetic state and had to confine myself in the youth hostel the entire day. At such a time as this, how I wished I had a fellow travelling companion to nurse me. I lay in bed and cried out to God to heal me and strengthen my limbs. God listened to my prayer: the day after, my strength was sufficiently renewed, and I visited the Natural History Museum of Zimbabwe.

The highlight of my visit to the museum was learning about Cecil Rhodes, a British mining businessman and politician in southern Africa. Back in my secondary school days, I had heard about Rhodes scholarship but did not know much about the person behind the scholarship. In this museum, there was a dedicated section about Rhodes' achievements and a room full of his memorabilia. From one of the exhibits, I copied this description in my diary:

> "The story of Rhodes is one of a man spurred on by ill-health to achieve in a short lifetime the stupendous works of a great chief. Some were successful – the foundation of Rhodesia and the great system of Rhodes Scholarships, some still await fulfillment – the federation of countries south of the Zambezi, and some have proved unnecessary – airways and radio have outmoded the Cape-to-Cairo railway and telegraph line... His whole life is summed up in a phrase from his will: 'to render myself useful to my country'."

Indeed, Rhodes contributed much to the political development of southern Africa. He became a member of the Cape Parliament at the age of 27 in 1880, and a decade later assumed the role of Prime Minister, overseeing the formation of Rhodesia in the early 1890s. He exercised his leadership for six years and was forced to resign in 1896 due to a political attack beyond his control. Plagued by years of poor health, he died in 1902 at a young age of 48. After viewing this section of the museum, I was more than convinced that it is not so much the length of one's life but the richness of one's experience that matters more. I was more motivated to lead a life filled with meaningful experiences.

One of the experiences I hoped to gain on this trip to Africa was to visit South Africa and see how apartheid was being practised. My two years in a British university thus far had exposed me to a number of unfair and discriminatory policies existing in this imperfect world. I was keen to personally experience life in a country where the whites and the blacks were segregated; I wondered how I, a Chinese, would be colour-coded. To enter South Africa, I needed a visa from the South African embassy in Harare, the capital city of Zimbabwe. With that in mind, I travelled in a north-easterly direction to Harare on a night train from Bulawayo. The journey took ten hours and I arrived as a new day dawned.

My time in Harare was non-descript. There was nothing particularly interesting that I encountered and experienced in this clean and modern city: I attended a Sunday service, visited the Queen Victoria Museum, and strolled in Africa Unity Park, a well-maintained garden in the middle of the city. I also bought some magazines to learn more about the local culture and politics, watched a movie and wrote some letters and postcards to friends. There was a certain lethargy hanging over me even as I acquainted myself with this new city. I did not actively think or sense that I was missing anything on this trip till I chanced upon a vegetable salad bar. For the first time since more than a month ago when I touched down at Nairobi airport, I tasted fresh vegetable salad. It was divine and heavenly!

Travelling solo had taught me to make plans but to also exercise flexibility when they did not turn out the way I imagined them to be. On the fourth morning in Harare, I hitched a ride from Dave, an American missionary in Zimbabwe, to the South African embassy. Upon arriving at the embassy at half past seven before the door opened, a queue measuring a few meters had already formed. I had to make a snap decision there and then. I could either stand in the queue to await my turn to apply for a South African visa, which might take more than a day, or abandon this plan for a visit to Malawi, which I heard through other travelers was well worth a trip. Dave was on his way to Kariba and could give me a lift that very morning, if I decided to go to Malawi through Kariba, a Zimbabwean border town with Zambia. Within a minute, I had the peace to give up the visit to South Africa and followed Dave to Kariba. A fellow solo German traveler, Matthias, also chose to come along. Unbeknownst to us, we were in for an unforgettable time at Kariba.

From Harare, the car headed in a north-westerly direction for about four hours before turning left at Makuti towards Kariba. This last stretch of road was meandering and mountainous and lasted about an hour. Dave dropped us off at Moth Holiday Resort where Matthias and I chose to camp at seven Zimbabwean dollars a night, about 2.2

British pounds. The facilities were decent for the price we paid. In the evening, we walked into a compound next to ours, Lion International, where a group of school children aged 7-12 were singing, led by an elderly white man and accompanied on guitar by a white young lady. That scene of white and black children sitting side by side warmed my heart. They seemed oblivious to all the fuss about skin color and co-existed harmoniously. Later, I learned that it was a camp organized by Scripture Union, a Christian organization. In my heart, I thanked God for bringing me here to witness the unity of black and white Zimbabwean children. It was certainly a better choice than seeing the segregation of these two colours in South Africa, where I had originally intended to go to.

Kariba was a place to relax and recharge for me. Nestled on the north-eastern bank of Lake Kariba, the biggest man-made lake in the world, the town felt like a seaside resort to me. I carried out my third laundry session since the beginning of my trip, and fed myself some good food such as bananas, pineapple and bread, and even cooked potatoes, onions, and beef steak. My body was regaining its strength and vitality; I was writing more in my diary. It was as though I was running the second half of a long race with second wind, and all things seemed bright and beautiful to me. Indeed, up at the observation point on Kariba Heights, where the huge Kariba dam could be reduced to a proportionate size before my eyes, the engineering feat of the dam was clearly stupendous. The resultant effects of a man-made lake and the many economic activities it afforded were truly amazing.

At Kariba, I was reminded that nature consisted of more than the sky, the mountains, and the lake, though together they formed a bucolic scene. Nature also includes animals that roam the land on which we live, and their need for food sometimes infringe upon our rights. Here, we witnessed five small wild elephants storming through plantations, helping themselves to whatever food they could forage. We also woke up one morning to find our bananas and pineapple missing from our campsite. Upon investigation, we were told by the lady running the campsite that it was not uncommon for wild monkeys to steal fruits from campers. This was comforting news. At least, we were assured that it was not a task accomplished by human hands --that would be more distressing!

On the whole, Kariba had a certain charm and gentility to it. I usually woke in the stillness of the morning when the sky was a pale sheet of blue and listened to the crisp chirping of the birds amongst the trees. Their refreshing tune would sometimes be interrupted by violent movements among the branches made by monkeys swinging from one branch to another. Once while I was staring meditatively at the vast blue sky, a mosquito with its wings fully spread hovered about six inches above me, as though reminding me of the beauty of its striped wings. I refused to pay it more attention and looked beyond this intruder, at a height hundreds of feet above where groups of birds flew in arrow formation. They delighted my eyes with their spectacular display of flying in unison; it was truly a mesmerizing scene that lifted my spirit, but alas, I was soon rudely interrupted and brought back to earth by the persistent barking of some deranged dogs.

Nature in Kariba was also about men having dominion over the fish of the lake. On a hot afternoon, while wandering rather aimlessly, we chanced upon a fishery and Matthias had this brilliant idea of going out on a commercial fishing boat with the fishermen. Thus, we walked into a fishery office to ask for permission, citing the intention to write an article on the fishing community as the reason. To our surprise, the manager of the fishery agreed, provided we signed an indemnity form absolving the company of any liability should we incur any injury or loss as a result of the trip. Unfortunately, we just missed the timing for that day. So we were determined to go on one the day after.

The overnight fishing trip was educational. I was fully awake throughout the night and recorded the activities with precise timings as follows:

3.45p.m.	departed in a fishing boat from Andorra Harbor with 3 black fishermen, all half-naked, and headed 25 km south.
6.20p.m.	sun had set, reached the destination where another fishing boat had already been stationed, waited to see the first catch of the other boat.
6.50p.m.	moved away from the first boat.
7.05p.m.	stopped, lowered the anchor, then the circular net with a light bulb was fully immersed.
9.05p.m.	net retrieved from the water, the catch of Kapenta (Tanganyika sardine) filled four rectangular boxes, salt sprinkled onto the fish to preserve them. Net and light bulb immersed again.
11.35p.m.	net retrieved the second time, the catch filled two boxes, also caught 3 big fish: 2 tigerfish and 1 barbel (catfish). Net and light bulb immersed again.

1.20 a.m.	net retrieved the third time, the catch filled one box, also caught 1 big fish. Boat moved to a new location.
5.40a.m.	net retrieved the fourth time, the catch filled twelve boxes, also caught 2 big fish. Water was getting choppy.
6.10 a.m.	moved to meet the other boat.
6.25 a.m.	sunrise, returned to Andorra Harbor; we were given a tigerfish.
7.00 a.m.	we were transferred onto another boat heading back to the harbor.
10.00a.m.	reached Andorra Harbor.

On this overnight fishing trip, I learned that commercial fishermen used a fish finder, a device for detecting fish underwater, to help them decide where to lower their nets, and a light bulb to attract the fish. In addition, they operated in pairs (two boats) so as to provide help to each other in case of emergency. I took many photos of the fishermen and promised to send them the pictures when I returned to England, which I did. Another interesting observation I had was that all fishermen were black Zimbabweans while their superiors in management positions were white Zimbabweans. This could be explained by the recent history of the country which used to be ruled by the minority white till 1980 when it gained independence. However, it would take a much longer time to see real social economic changes between the two peoples, perhaps after one to two generations.

The five days I spent in Kariba were restorative. I had fully recovered from the frailty experienced in

Bulawayo and to some extent in Harare. I enjoyed the gentility and quietude of Kariba and had a lot of time to get close to nature in the form of scenery and animals. In particular, the overnight fishing trip was a real treat as I had not experienced anything like this before, not even in Singapore or Malaysia. Above all, I cherished the sight of black and white Zimbabwean children singing and worshipping God together; the sight signaled hope for the country. Like multi-cultural Singapore, future generations of Zimbabweans could strive to live and work together in harmony regardless of skin color. It was with such a hope for the country that I left Zimbabwe for Malawi. To get to Malawi from Kariba, I needed to pass through Lusaka and Chipata in Zambia. I was given four days at the Zambia Immigration at Kariba Road Barrier to transit the country. In my mind, it would be an easy passage, but was I absolutely misguided in my assumption!

The passage through Zambia turned out to be drama in its most intense form. I managed to secure a lift to Lusaka quite easily. In the space of about three hours, I found myself in the capital city of Zambia where I exchanged the remaining ten Zimbabwean dollars for fifty Zambian kwachas. With that amount, I bought some snacks and continued to hitch rides going in a westerly direction, hoping to arrive at Chipata at the end of the day. However, after three short rides, I managed to reach only Chongwe, some fifty odd kilometers from Lusaka. It was here that I waited in vain for hours, till the sun was about to set. A kind-hearted young man Charles then came to my rescue, bringing me to his brother-in-law's house where I spent a night free of charge. I was hungry, surviving on only some bread and a cup of tea for dinner;

still, I was thankful to God for sending an angel to provide me with free lodging for the night.

I began the next morning with renewed hope. Charles out of his natural goodness blessed me with ten kwachas to buy some food on my journey. Without waiting for too long, I managed to get two short rides covering a total of about 30 kilometers. It was half past ten in the morning then, and I was hopeful of making it to Chipata or even crossing the border into Malawi by the end of the day. But hours after hours I waited by the side of the road and no car stopped to pick me up; my patience and hope soon gave way to frustration and anger as the daylight faded in the dusk. At the suggestion of a local traveler, I went with him to seek shelter at his friend's place. We were both hungry and tired after standing by the side of a road for hours, and really appreciated the hospitality of the friend who served us tea and some buns.

Just as we finished our food, two men rushed into the small dim room. One of them was particularly harsh in his tone as he interrogated me. He demanded to know every single detail of my journey from Zimbabwe to Chongwe, and how I managed to get into the house I was in. To put it bluntly, I was accused of being a spy in Zambia! To these two men, I was one of the whites whose abominable activities had resulted in the death of many Zambians. My baggage was thoroughly searched; every item in it was examined and re-examined; my passport was closely scrutinized. Finding nothing suspicious, the two men then made a big fuss about my army-issued water bottle, which according to them would have unimaginable implications and consequences. Upon hearing my explanation that every young man in my country had to serve national service, one of them quickly implicated that I was army-trained and thereby 'army-conscious', making me a likely spy.

After almost two hours of interrogation, during which he spoke aggressively when making certain accusation to which I tried not to rebut, his voice became more subdued and friendly. Out of the blue, he told me that he did not hate me, which moments ago he blatantly professed. On learning that I am a Chinese, I was accorded the respect due to the Chinese from China who had rendered great help to Zambia through the Tazara project. He then offered to take me to a nearby police station to spend the night, where I would be able to rest in safety, and promised me that the policemen would be able to arrange a lift to Malawi for me the next day. I thanked him and followed him. In my heart, I thanked God that the interrogation was over and that I was found innocent.

In a corner of the police station, I unrolled my sleeping mat and sleeping bag and willingly came under the custody of the Zambian police for a night.

CHAPTER 8

Travelling from Malawi to Masai Mara

Those who hope in the Lord will renew their strength. They will soar on wings like eagles; they will run and not grow weary; they will walk and not be faint.

Isaiah 40:31

God works in marvelous ways. His ways are not our ways; His ways are always higher than our ways. After a seemingly god-forsaken day the day before, everything fell into place very neatly. As promised, the police at Chongwe managed to arrange a lift for me early the next morning. The driver, a military policeman, brought me all the way to Chipata, covering a distance of 530 kilometers in about seven hours. And the best part of it was that I did not have to pay at all! At Chipata bus station, I jumped onto a pick-up that was heading towards the Zambian border. After clearing the immigration, I paid five Zambian kwachas to traverse through the 12 kilometers of no man's land between the two countries.

Upon clearing the Malawian immigration at Mchinji, I managed to negotiate for a lift to Lilongwe, the capital city of Malawi, for five Malawian kwachas (which was slightly more than one British pound). The 125-kilometer journey took about two hours, at the end of which the sun was setting over the land. I was glad to check into a guesthouse at Lilongwe. Incidentally, the name of the guesthouse was 'Feel At Home Rest House'. How aptly it described my feelings then, considering that I was rudely interrogated and had to spend the previous night at a police station in Zambia. Figuratively, the smooth entry into Malawi was, to me, the calm after a storm.

The calm in Lilongwe soon turned into excitement. Much to my surprise the following day, I came across a Chinese shop near the guesthouse with big Chinese characters in traditional script written on the wall outside the shop. I wondered who the Chinese words were meant for since most people in Malawi would not be able to read Chinese. In front of the wall were three handsome young African men behind three sewing machines, all hard at work. A wooden bench was placed before the second machine, and a teenage boy, presumably a customer, was sitting on it. I was intrigued by this accidental discovery and entered the shop to find out more. In my limited knowledge of African politics, I had not learned about Taiwanese economic influence in Malawi.

The owner of the shop was a Taiwanese farmer who had relocated to Malawi for some years. Mr Zhuang, as he introduced himself, was also delighted to see me, a Chinese from Singapore. In fact, he was so hospitable that he invited me to have lunch and later dinner with him. It was heavenly to taste Chinese food once again after one and a half months of African food and snacks. I was filled with thanksgiving to God. On top of that, Mr Zhuang also offered to house me at his farm, some 16 kilometers outside of Lilongwe. Enroute to his farm, we stopped at a garden where I took a photograph of four African boys sitting on a small bridge with a Chinese pagoda in the background. The garden was a donation by the Taiwanese government to Malawi, I was told. In my mind, I could not make sense of this political gesture by the Taiwanese government until much later: While China was making generous contributions to Tanzania and Zambia through the building of the Tazara railway, Taiwan was courting the friendship of Malawi. It was a competition in winning African nations to support its own political agenda in the United Nations (UN), especially after China was voted in and Taiwan expelled from the UN on 25 October, 1971.

Mr Zhuang owned a poultry farm which employed a number of local workers. Through our conversation, I learned through him that Africans had no concept of saving and apportioning money. When he first arrived, he used to dispense salaries to his workers on a monthly basis. Then to his horror, a few days after payday, he discovered that his workers had no more money left; they had spent their salaries on drinks and entertainment. Subsequently, he had to educate them to give a portion of the money to their wives and to save for rainy days. He also implemented a half-monthly salary payment for his workers so that they were paid more frequently and had less money to handle each time, which would help them manage their resources in a more responsible way and not squander them in a few days.

In view of the fact that I had another month to spend in Africa, I decided to linger one more day at Mr Zhuang's farm, with his permission. I wanted to slow down, consolidate my thoughts, and plan my Malawian itinerary by reading the Lonely Planet guidebook on Africa. Also, I wanted to count my blessings and share them with my sister in Singapore in the form of a letter, in which I narrated my exciting overnight outing with the fishermen on Lake Kariba and my ordeal while trying to pass through Zambia, giving thanks to God for His wonderful provision. I ended the letter by sharing with her how the series of events had brought me a step closer to understanding the word of God in Matthew 6, verses 25-34, which in essence is about abandoning our anxieties and trusting in God.

After two nights at the farm, I was refreshed, rejuvenated and determined to head south towards the Mulanje mountains. The morning of my departure from the farm, I followed Mr Zhuang back to his house in Lilongwe for a Chinese breakfast. It could possibly be my last Chinese meal on this continent, and I savored every bite of it. In return, I gave him a Good News Bible as a souvenir and thanked him profusely for his hospitality. To him, I must be a random overseas Chinese that happened to cross his path in Malawi; to me, he was a godsend at a time of need for rest and restoration; and to God, he must be a beloved whom God wanted to bless, and I was the bearer of His good news. Anyway, Mr Zhuang readily accepted the Bible and gave me a lift to the bus station.

The bus schedule in Malawi was unreliable and erratic. My journey from Lilongwe to Mulanje covering less than 400 kilometres had to be done in stages and took me two days. First, I had to get from Lilongwe to Blantyre, covering 320 kilometres in nine slow and painful hours; then after an overnight stay at Blantyre, I had to wait about six hours for an express bus to Mulanje. To exacerbate the delay, the bus broke down soon after it started running, testing and stretching my patience further with another wait for a replacement bus. This experience strengthened my resolve to travel via steamers on Lake Malawi as far as possible. Even though I had a lot of time in Africa, I had no desire to spend it on waiting for buses or for them to be repaired every now and then along the bumpy and pothole-ridden roads.

My attempt to trek in the Mulanje mountains got off to a good start. After my morning quiet time with the Lord and a shower, I managed to hitch a ride to the Likabula Forest Station, some 15 kilometres away. Having consulted the office personnel and finding out more information from the noticeboard, I hired a 16-year-old porter-cum-guide, Romous, who could understand and speak some basic English. It was not so much a porter that I needed but some company along this two-day trek. According to the route I had selected, I paid for two nights of hut fees costing a total of 5 Malawian kwachas, and at the end of the trek would have to pay my porter Romous 19 Malawian kwachas.

One of the advantages of hiring a local porter was the privilege of gaining a glimpse into the culture of the local people in the Mulanje mountains. Romous brought me to the local market where he bought some salt and dried fish for the trek; then he brought me back to his home which was a four by two-metre mud hut topped with straws. Like him, his younger siblings all did not wear any shoes or slippers but went about bare-footed. They all seemed adequately fed and contented. Before we set off for the mountains, we had a typical local lunch consisting of nsima (a staple made from maize flour), kapenta (a kind of local fish) and okra (a kind of vegetable that resembles ladies' fingers). It was simple and delicious.

The trek from Likabula Forest Station to Chambe Hut was a three-hour climb, and in the process, we gained more than one thousand meters in vertical distance. Due to the afternoon heat, Romous soon removed his T-shirt and secured it to my backpack which he was carrying; I followed him from a distance, stopping occasionally to capture a shot of the mountains. Once every so often, we passed by individuals walking sure-footedly down the mountain, balancing one or two long planks of wood on their heads. These people were paid to carry planks, sawn and prepared up in the mountains, down to the villages where they would be used to build houses. Coming from Singapore, a seaport, I was familiar with the term 'coolies' being used to describe labourers who carried heavy loads onto and off the boats; here in the Mulanje mountains, however, coolies carried planks of wood downhill. I was thrilled to think that nature not only provided materials for mankind to build houses but also employment for these Mulanje coolies, including my young porter.

Part of the joy of climbing mountains is the opportunity to watch a spectacular sunrise from an elevated position. For this reason, I instructed Romous to wake me at 4 o'clock the next morning so that we could catch the sunrise at Chambe Peak (2557m), another two hours of trekking from Chambe Hut (1844m). My porter did wake me the next morning, but it was forty minutes later than planned. After putting on a jumper and my hiking boots, I signaled for him to lead the way while I followed from behind. The wind was howling rather fiercely and to my amazement, I saw that he had only a thin T-shirt on his body and no shoes on his feet. Sensing his need, I offered him my windbreaker; as for shoes, I had no spare ones for him to use. He gladly accepted the windbreaker and put it on. In the stillness of the early morning, under sufficient lighting of the full moon, we braved the cold and trekked briskly up the mountain.

Romous impressed me with his agility and speed. Despite the cold—or was it because of it—he was fleet-footed and many a time, he was a dark shifting shadow some five to ten metres ahead of me. I tried my best to focus my eyes on him so that I would not lose him. At the same time, I was intent on capturing the beauty of the break of dawn as the sky brightened slowly, allowing streaks of light to glow weakly in the distance as though they were struggling to break free of the dominion of the huge mountain range. It was a rare sight, a precious glimpse of nature in tussle, of light overcoming darkness. As we ascended further, visibility became obscured as the clouds swept past us swiftly, sending chills down my spine, literally and figuratively. In such adverse conditions, Romous soldiered on bare-footed, in search of the peak.

Chambe Peak finally came into sight. At its highest point (2557m), a two-metre cylindrical metal structure was erected to inform trekkers that they had arrived at the peak; it was not a beautiful monument. And the poor visibility then did not afford us a panoramic view of the surrounding. Nevertheless, I was glad that we made it in good time: 1 hour and 45 minutes. Without much delay, I gestured to Romous to sit down for breakfast; he had carried in a small food bag some bananas, biscuits and groundnuts which provided us with some energy. Before we left the peak, I asked Romous to take a picture of me seated in front of the cylindrical structure, my arms folded due to the cold. The photograph did not turn out sharp as the misty clouds were all around me. Nevertheless, it is a record of my sincere mountaineering exploit in Malawi.

Extra precaution was exercised in our descent. Cognizant of the steep slopes, and the possibilities of slipping, I asked Romous to move at a leisurely pace. At various junctures, I enforced stoppages as I paused to take photos of the surrounding mountains. This explained why we took as long to descend as it took us to ascend the peak. Upon returning to Chambe Hut, we had slices of pineapple which were refreshing both to the mouth and to the spirit. We spent the rest of the morning walking around the clearing in the midst of tall pine trees, looking at how the locals produce charcoal in spherical kilns made of bricks. It was a kind of work which required a lot of waiting—waiting for the wood fed into the kilns to become charcoal black. In the process of waiting, some workers were playing a kind of African board game. The board was a thick piece of unvarnished solid wood with many holes dug into it, and small marbles were either added or subtracted from the holes by the players. From the faces of the players, I could tell that they were truly enjoying the game.

After a simple lunch, we left Chambe Hut for Lichenya Hut. In terms of elevation, both were situated at about 1840 meters above the sea level; however, in terms of distance, they were about 3 hours of walking apart from each other. We did not rush as we did in the early morning; there were plenty of daylight hours. At one point, I took longer than usual to take photographs of the surrounding mountains as I needed to look for a shady place to remove a roll of colour film from my camera and put into it a new roll of black and white film. Romous sat in a corner, waiting rather impatiently. As it turned out, the effects of the black and white photographs were more authentic and classic; they captured the layers of mountains in the background and the different shades of green of the foreground more distinctly. We reached Lichenya Hut in the late afternoon where I got someone to take a photograph of Romous and me standing in front of the hut. He wrote his mailing address in my diary and I promised to send him the photos upon my return to England.

The next morning, our trek from Lichenya Hut (1843m) to Likubula Forest Station (775m) was rather effortless since it was downhill most of the way. However, I did come across something unusual. We met four young porters around Romous' age who were heading in the opposite direction, and what they were carrying intrigued me: two were each carrying a basket full of items while the other two were each holding onto a white child on their shoulders. The parents of these small children were nowhere in sight, probably trailing far behind. I took a shot of the four porters and their loads, marveling at the level of trust these parents had in the four boy porters, who probably moved at a pace that was too fast for the adults. Anyway, the two children seemed to enjoy riding on the backs of their porters.

Back at Likubula Forest Station, I bade Romous farewell. I paid him 22 kwachas—three more than the official -- for his service and gave him a pair of my army shorts. I also asked him to inform me of his school results when they became available. He did. More than a month later, back in England, I received a letter from him informing me that he did well enough to gain admission into a secondary school. More importantly, he asked for financial assistance; I sent him my remaining 20 Malawian kwachas which I had intended to keep as a souvenir, and two postcard-size photos of him and his house. It was the least I could do for my porter.

My journey from Mulanje to Monkey Bay was perfectly timed, and I thanked God for it. Immediately after bidding farewell to my porter, I managed to hitch a ride for about 30 kilometres before catching a bus to Limbe, where I connected a bus bound for Monkey Bay, some 260 kilometres to the north on the southern tip of Lake Malawi. Arriving in the late afternoon, I checked into Monkey Bay Rest House and had the intention to travel in one of the two steamers mentioned in my guidebook plying the elongated lake. Going by the published schedule, I would be travelling in MV Ilala which would depart from Monkey Bay every Friday morning. That left me with one full day to rest and recover from my trek on the Mulanje mountains. I used this day to write several postcards to friends and family members, including one to the Booklesses and a letter to the Crowhursts, my spiritual mentors, back in England. I shared with them the highlights of my travel thus far and concluded that God is good despite the fact that we may sometimes be afflicted with some sufferings.

I was all excited to board the ship MV Ilala on Friday morning and to spend the next two days sailing on it. Having been forewarned by the guidebook that second and third class ticket holders would be packed like sardines at the lowest deck, I bought a first class ticket without a cabin (sleep on deck) bound for Nkhata Bay, about two-third way up the lake, for 108.50 Malawian kwachas, which was equivalent to 23 British pounds. It was the perfect choice as there was plenty of deck space, and with a good sleeping bag, I was kept sufficiently warm at night; in addition, when darkness had blanketed the entire lake, my mind was kept occupied by the brilliance of the clusters of stars hanging above me, with each constellation telling its own story of origin. This visual feast would not be available for first-class cabin passengers, whose costlier tickets confined them to small cubicles in the vessel.

The ferry Ilala called at many ports on its way up Lake Malawi. At each port, there was a stopover time of at least half an hour or more for passengers to disembark and embark. At some ports where the water was too shallow for the ferry to dock, it had to drop its anchor about 100 meters from the shore, and the stopover time was therefore longer. Small wooden boats, each carrying a few passengers and their baskets of poultry and sacks of agricultural produce, would be lowered into the water and carry disembarking passengers to shore while passengers waiting at the shore would load themselves onto these small boats to board the ferry; each boat was being paddled by two or more persons onboard. At the second stop at Makanjila, a fishing village, where we were going to stop for 90 minutes, I decided to go on shore to see the village.

What really caught my attention on the beach of Makanjila was the sight of a dugout canoe, a boat made from a single tree trunk that had been hollowed. Curiosity brought me nearer to the canoe, and then I found myself engaged in a friendly deal:

"Hello! Can you snap me one picture?" A young man asked me.

"Hm…Ok! But after that, can you send me back to the ferry in your canoe?"

"Ok! No problem."

"Alright, smile…" I took a photo of him and his friends beside the canoe.

"Thank you! Can you send to me?"

"Sure, sure! In October." I readily agreed to his request.

"Ok, now, let's go." He motioned for me to sit down on the canoe.

"Yes… but how do you sit on it?" I asked as there was not enough room for me to put my legs into the canoe.

"Just sit, it is ok. No problem." He reassured me and demonstrated how to do it.

So I sat precariously on the canoe rather than in it, facing the shore while three of them sat in a straight line facing me. There was so much joy on their faces as two of them paddled the canoe towards the ferry. I captured their smiley faces in a black and white photograph which, together with the one taken earlier, was sent to the young man a month later. The ride on the canoe was an unforgettable experience which I still treasure in my heart.

Another memorable sighting on this ferry trip was that of a baobab tree on Likoma Island, a small island in the middle of Lake Malawi that belongs to Malawi though it is geographically located closer to Mozambique. I first learned about this tree in my secondary two Geography class; I never dreamed at that time that I would one day visit Africa and see this tree for myself. A symbol of life in a harsh landscape, the baobab tree is able to absorb and store water in its broad trunk during the rainy season, thus enabling it to produce a nutrient-rich fruit in the dry season when all around is dry and arid. Its fruits not only serve as food for many animals but are also beneficial for human consumption, promoting physical health and enhancing body immunity. For this reason, the tree is aptly known as the tree of life in Africa. The sighting of this tree reminded me of God's goodness in giving me an opportunity to visit Africa; it also caused me to see God's hand of provision in a dry and weary land.

On board Ilala, I had plenty of time to reflect on life. The stark inequality of life hit home on board the ferry where first class passengers occupied the second and top decks, leaving the second-class and third-class passengers to jostle for space in the lower deck. It was a classic illustration of 20 percent of the population owning 80 percent of the absolute wealth of a given country or community. People are often stratified according to wealth, and sometimes this invariably means according to racial or ethnic divide in some countries. Also, one's perspective of life depends on the vantage point from which one looks at an issue. For example, from the top deck, the vast expanse of water around me looked relatively calm like gentle ripples breaking forth; however, from the lower deck, one could hear the waters beating relentlessly against the sides of the ferry and sense that all was not so tranquil.

Watching the sun set and rise from the ferry, I also concluded that precision of time was a meaningless construct in Africa. Unlike life in England or Singapore, where life was regulated by precise timings, here in the middle of a lake in Africa, time was measured by the position of the sun and the length of a shadow it cast. The exact hour and minutes were not important; estimates sufficed. Time just slipped by subtly and imperceptibly, even as the scenery changed quite unnoticeably. And when complete darkness enveloped the entire lake, there was no necessity to figure out the line that separated the sky and the water; the knowledge that the two elements were out there in the darkness was enough. Precision was not a necessity; estimates were good enough for work to be done, sufficient for life to keep rolling on, albeit slowly. As I reflected on this, I concluded that one should not treat any one of the concepts of time as superior to another; instead, one needed to adapt and respond accordingly when operating in a different culture.

Amongst the foreigners seen on the first-class deck were some white South Africans, a young German couple, and Nina, a Swiss lady travelling by herself. On the second evening, an elderly white South African couple kindly invited both Nina and I to have dinner with them in the small restaurant on board Ilala. It was an unexpected treat and I enjoyed the company and the food. Their hospitality reminded me of my spiritual parents back in Loughborough who once every so often invited foreign students to dine with them. I was thankful for the Western meal and the little wine that came with it; it was a meaningful celebration to round off the two-day voyage on Ilala.

The land journey from Nkhata Bay to Livingstonia measuring 175 kilometers was fraught with uncertainties as the public transport was less than reliable. Since Nina was also alighting at Nkhata Bay and heading towards Livingstonia, we decided to travel together for that stretch of road. We had to take short rides to Mzuzu and then to Rumphi and finally to Livingstonia. In between, there was a lot of waiting. It was good that Nina and I kept each other company while waiting. We discussed issues pertaining to Israel and many other topics related to politics. Perhaps somewhere during our discourse, my ignorance of some historical events was blatantly revealed, so much so that when I came across a bookshop selling some history textbooks at Mzuzu, I bought two to help me understand world history better. Certainly, I was also interested to know more about the history of African countries, especially those that I had visited.

Livingstonia was worth a visit due to its historical significance despite the irregularity of transport. Perched on a high ground some 900 meters above Lake Malawi, and linked to the main north-south highway through a 16-kilometer stretch of winding road that consists of 20 hairpin bends, the town is a testimony of the good work done by the Scottish missionaries. Following the death of Dr David Livingstone in 1873, there was a concerted effort to boost mission work in eastern Africa. One of Livingstone's disciples, Dr Robert Laws, spent 52 years in this country, including 50 years as the head of the Livingstonia Mission. He built a stone house in Livingstonia in 1903 and lived in it for 25 years. Being an educationist at heart, he also established a school and a technical training centre in this town, in addition to a hospital and a church. Much of what he achieved still survives to this day.

We were fortunate to arrive at Livingstonia at half past four in the afternoon, an hour before sunset. Together with two New Zealander ladies whom we met along the way, we checked into the Stone House, which had been turned into a hotel offering food and lodging to visitors. All four of us chose to camp rather than to sleep in rooms in order to save cost; we slept along the veranda, in our sleeping bags which protected us from the wind. We each paid 5 kwachas for camping and another 2 kwachas for dinner. The best bargain was the fact that we could use the common bathroom in the house, and it came with a bathtub! It was a luxury I had not dreamt of when I considered travelling in Africa. The dinner, the warm bath, and the cool air out in the veranda combined to induce sleep in me.

The next morning, shortly after five o'clock, I woke to a view that was magnificent and breathtaking in proportion. Roused to consciousness by a cacophony of bucolic sounds, which included the crowing of cockerels and the barking of dogs, I opened my eyes slowly to find the sun already emitting faint traces of light in the sky. The clouds were colored in a mixture of white, blue, pink and red, floating by as though to invite me to take in the beauty of the undulating landscape in front of me. My heart was gladdened by the beauty before me, and I immediately took out my diary to record the scene in words, so that in the years ahead I might relive this joyous moment and fill my heart with pleasure once again, like Wordsworth did with the sight of the dancing daffodils in his famous poem, *I Wandered Lonely as a Cloud*.

The dream-like trance I was in was soon interrupted by the stirring of Nina who was waking. She got out of her sleeping bag and was beginning to pack and leave Livingstonia for Zimbabwe. Thankful for her company in the past few days, I decided to get up and walk her to the roundabout where she could wait for a ride downhill. To be honest, I felt a tinge of sadness that we had to go our separate ways. To bid her farewell, I gave her the blessings of God in the form of two booklets entitled 'The Gospel of John' and 'Caring', trusting that they would draw her closer to the mysteries and love of God.

Back in the Stone House, I found something meaningful to occupy my mind so that I would not dwell on the sadness brought about by Nina's departure. Next to the house was a small but fascinating museum about the history of Livingstonia. It contained records of the first European arrivals in Malawi and the first missionaries in the forms of old photographic prints, wall displays, furniture and equipment dating from the earliest times of the establishment of the mission. I was particularly captured by the display of a pendulum clock in a glass casing which was presented to Margaret Gray and Robert Laws on the occasion of their wedding in July 1879. It was still ticking with pinpoint accuracy! In one of the quotations on the walls of the museum, I noted one of the aspirations of Dr Laws based on the teaching in Ephesians 2:14 in the Bible: "...the people of Livingstonia were able to tell the world that it was possible, through the love of Christ, to live together in harmony, even in times of tension." The message of unity was powerful for the different African tribes as well as between the white European missionaries and the local people.

My time in Livingstonia was short but it was well worth it. I had been given a glimpse of the missionary efforts of Dr Robert Laws and many others who followed in his footsteps. They served with dedication and perseverance, and their service was often sprinkled with a lot of joy and personal sacrifices. For example, it was recorded that Dr Laws was instrumental in founding some 700 schools and training centers all over the country, and he ordained many African pastors; however, it was also true that he and his wife had eight children but only one daughter, Amelia Nyasa Laws, survived. His 52 years of faithful and fruitful service in Central Africa was and still is an inspiration to all budding missionaries the world over.

On this high note of service and dedication I left Livingstonia. After writing and sending a postcard to my sister back in Singapore at the local post office, I managed to flag down a sand truck heading downhill and paid the driver 1.5 kwachas for the 16-kilometer journey. Another bus journey then brought me to Karonga, 90 kilometers further north, where I spent a night before boarding another bus to Songwe, the last village of Malawi on the northern border with Tanzania. The immigration officer was nonchalant about his job; he placed a weak stamp in my passport, signed on it and let me through without any questioning. I crossed the border, demarcated by a bridge over a river, by foot and entered Tanzania for the second time.

In contrast, the officers at the Tanzanian immigration scrutinized me and inspected my baggage. For reasons that were not made known to me, they confiscated a magazine on South Africa. I did not argue but was just glad that I was allowed through the immigration. With intermittent waiting along the way, during which I tried to exchange Malawian kwachas into Tanzanian shillings with some locals, I found my way to Kyela, and then to Mbeya, a major city in southwest Tanzania, after sunset. With only 20 shillings in my pocket, I could not check into a guest house but was glad to be led by a kind soul to a waiting room at a bus station for bus passengers where I spent the night free of charge. I bought a cup of tea and two tiny buns to fill my stomach. Then, under pairs of curious and unbelieving eyes, I unrolled my sleeping mat and sleeping bag, removed my walking boots, slipped into the bag and began writing my diary. It had been a tough day travelling on the road with little food, but I thanked God for helping me to overcome the difficulties with whatever little money I had on me. Just before I fell asleep, I thought of Nina and prayed for her to be wise, to depend on God's strength and wisdom.

The next morning, I awoke once again to pairs of curious eyes straining on me as I slipped out of my sleeping bag. They must be surprised to see a 'homeless' foreigner spending a night in a public space such as a waiting room in a bus station. Although I had not been attending Sunday church services regularly as I travelled, I had been keeping my habit of reading the Bible each morning whenever possible. That morning, my reading brought me to the ninth chapter of the book of Acts, which is about the conversion of Saul along the road to Damascus. I marveled at the hand of God which orchestrated Saul's conversion by first blinding him and then sending a disciple named Ananias to restore his sight. I was particularly struck by the obedience of Ananias who, despite his initial fear, went to lay his hand on Saul and baptized him. Ananias' faith in God was manifested through his obedience to carry out God's instructions to him; indeed, faith must be backed by actions. The word of God that morning inspired me to journey on in faith.

A visit to the bank to exchange 10 British pounds into Tanzanian shillings afforded me the fare to book a bus seat bound for Dar es Salaam. It departed Mbeya at about 2 p.m. and took 20 hours to reach Dar es Salaam, covering a distance of 812 kilometers. I was by then used to long bus or train journeys in Africa and did not mind the discomfort of spending a night on the bus. Instead, my main concern was safety, considering the fact that most buses were old and often broke down in the middle of nowhere. Thus, I was relieved when the bus finally pulled into Dar es Salaam at about 10 o'clock the next morning.

Having travelled through Zimbabwe and Malawi, which were more orderly and less congested, I was repelled by the sight of Dar es Salaam, entering it the second time. The haphazardness of its buildings, the chaos of the traffic, the pollution of the air, and the unbearable heat, they had the effect of urging me to leave the city as soon as possible. But I did not wish to continue my journey in a bus. Thus, I hopped over to the train station just opposite the road. With the help of a railway staff, I managed to secure a second-class train ticket for Tanga leaving that afternoon. What a relief it was to have settled my onward journey; after that, I left the station in search for some food to strengthen myself.

Back at Dar es Salaam railway station, I was to witness a scene filled with anger and chaos. The passengers were angry that the train was late and that they were not allowed onto the platform. The policemen, on the other hand, were furious at the unruly behavior of the crowd and slammed the gate shut. Naturally, there was a heated verbal exchange of words (which I did not understand) with faces displaying heightened emotions and gestures running wild. After what seemed like eternity, the gate was finally unlocked, and the masses rushed to board the train. There was no organization and many passengers simply occupied whatever seats they could find in the carriages. This resulted in a commotion when the ticket inspector undertook the hassle of sorting these people out. What a whole lot of noise and confusion! After what seemed an eternity, the train finally pulled out of the station at 5.15p.m. Soon, the sky fell into dark oblivion, and human noises gave way to the droning sound of the carriage wheels running rhythmically on the railway tracks, lulling some people into deep sleep.

The train pulled into Tanga station at 7.10 a.m. after almost 14 hours. As I was running short of Tanzanian shillings, it was in my interest to cross the border into Kenya soon. After some enquiries at the railway police station, I found my way to the city bus station. However, with only 200 shillings left in my possession, I did not have enough local money to buy a bus ticket to Mombasa in Kenya. To go to the bank to encash my Traveller's Cheques would mean missing the bus and being delayed for a day, which I was not inclined to do. Just then, I picked up courage to talk to some passengers at the station, explaining my need for a little money to travel to Mombasa. All praise be to God -- one kind soul offered me 200 shillings! With 400 shillings, I bought a bus ticket and departed for Mombasa in the late morning of the same day. Once again, I had experienced God's goodness and provision for me.

The bus journey from Tanga to Mombasa covering 176 kilometres took up the entire afternoon. The stretch of road leading to the border between Tanzania and Kenya at Lungalunga was really scenic. The land was green and fertile, and to some extent wild. Coconut trees in particular pre-dominated the landscape, and small clusters of mud huts appeared at irregular intervals. Some women and children could be seen relaxing themselves outside their huts. On many occasions, I waved at them and saw the children waving back fervently, shouting and laughing away as they did. There was gaiety and spontaneity in their gestures, and the immaculate whiteness of their teeth juxtaposed and contrasted perfectly with the darkness of their faces. Such occurrences spiced up the monotony of sitting hours in a bus.

It was a relief for me to reach Mombasa, a coastal city fronting the Indian Ocean and the second biggest city in

Kenya. I would be flying back to England from Nairobi, the capital city of this country, in about two weeks' time. Not only did I not have to concern myself with more currency exchange as there were no more international borders to cross, I could use up the rest of my Traveller's Cheques amounting to 150 British pounds in Kenya since this country would be my last stop. More importantly, my arrival in Mombasa meant that I could finally have a hot-water shower and a good night of rest in a guesthouse after being constantly on the move in the last few days. The past four nights spent at Karonga (a border town in Malawi), Mbeya bus station (a city in south-west Tanzania), on an overnight bus to Dar es Salaam, and on an overnight train to Tanga had been rough and hurried. In Mombasa, it was heavenly to feel clean once again, and to be able to do my final round of laundry!

Mombasa struck me as a city for tourists. In the city center, almost every street was filled with shops selling handicrafts or souvenirs. Along Moi Avenue, there were two huge structures in the form of two pairs of elephant tusks erected in the middle of the road, to commemorate the visit of Queen Elizabeth in 1952 when Kenya was still a British colony. I also ventured to the old port of Mombasa and found the area very filthy. The narrow streets and alleys and the surrounding Arabic structures reminded me of Old Jaffa port in Israel. As I popped into some shops to enquire the prices of some souvenir items, I discovered that shops in the city center were quoting rip-off prices, and as a foreigner, I needed to exercise my negotiation skills – bargaining.

From Mombasa, I took short excursions to smaller coastal towns. Remembering how Bagamoyo was so much more interesting than the bigger city of Dar es

Salaam in Tanzania, I headed northeast along the Kenyan coast to Malindi, a beach resort some 120 kilometers from Mombasa and spent two days there. I took a leisurely stroll along the beach in Malindi and also visited the monument put up by Vasco Da Gama, a Portuguese explorer and the first European to reach India by sea.

On the second day, I took a day trip to Watamu, a small village some 16 kilometers south of Malindi and saw a group of young men clearing seaweeds on the beach in front of Watamu Beach Hotel, a large and posh hotel. The thick layers of seaweed were brought onshore during high tide but they were left behind when the tide receded. In order to maintain its pristine beach condition, the hotel employed locals to clean the beach each morning. This is how nature provides employment, even though a daily wage of 32 Kenyan shillings was rather low.

In a separate incident, God spoke to me through a most unusual incident in Watamu. After lunch, as I settled down at a high spot to write cards and letters to friends, a little goat whose entire head was caught in a big tin can appeared in front of me. This poor creature could not see as its tiny horn was stuck in the can, preventing it from extricating its head from the can. I found the sight amusing and took a photo of it. Just as I was about to go away, I heard an inner voice telling me to help this poor creature. I did. Without much trouble, I managed to set it free and restore its sight. Instantly, it began to move towards the other goats, bleating with joy as it leaped away. The other goats also bleated, as though celebrating and rejoicing with the former in its release from bondage.

A divine interpretation of this incident came to mind almost immediately after the little goat had been set free. The poor creature was like a man in his helpless state. Just as the other goats could not help this little one remove the can from its head, so men sometimes could not help a fellow human being in a dire situation. It takes a being greater than the goat to set it free; likewise, it takes a being greater than man to rescue him. In the incident, it was so simple for me to set the little goat free; similarly, in many dire situations, it must be so easy for God to set men free, if only men would willingly accept His help. The goat was wise not to resist my attempt to help it out of the trap. In the same way, men could be wise by not rejecting but accepting God's grace and love. I thanked God for this revelation. Indeed, I thanked God for His amazing grace upon me.

Together with a fellow solo traveller from Germany whom I met in Malindi, I returned to Mombasa the next morning. Since I would be flying back to England soon, I took the liberty to buy some souvenirs: I traded my Lacoste T-shirt for two small Masai wood carvings, in addition to paying a small sum of 30 Kenyan shillings and giving the shopkeeper a gift in the form of a London postcard. I also bought a collection of African prose and poetry for 30 Kenyan shillings, and an old map of the African continent on a bark cloth for 50 Kenyan shillings. These were to adorn my room back in Loughborough and serve as memories of my wandering in Africa. I was truly satisfied with my purchases and could not wait to share them with my friends back in Loughborough.

I purchased a third-class ticket for a night train from Mombasa to Nairobi, my last stop in this entire journey. The train was late, but it did not frustrate me as I had gotten used to such delays after spending more than two months in Africa. I simply waited, like the locals, from 7p.m. to 2.45a.m. when the train finally departed.

Enroute, the train passed through Tsavo National Park and I spotted some giraffes, zebras and ostriches in the distant grasslands, as well as some Masai herding cattle. It was nature in its most natural and unspoiled form. I told myself that I would like to book a safari tour once I arrived at Nairobi, if time and finances allowed me to do so.

God must have heard the desire of my heart. Without me deliberately searching for a safari tour operator, the next day I ran into one who was divinely placed at Iqbal Hotel, a stone's throw from my guesthouse. He was there to meet some customers, and upon my inquiry for a tour that would take place the following day, he brought me to his office, Exotic Safaris, where I made payment for a five-day camping safari, departing the very next morning to Lake Nakuru National Park and Masai Mara National Reserve. He assured me that the company was a reliable tour operator and that I had been given a generous discount which I should not disclose to other campers.[23] The entire incident happened so neatly and smoothly that I could only attribute it to God's hand perfecting the transaction.

On Day 1, I was picked up by a driver and his co-worker (a cook) at my guesthouse. Apart from me, there were three other individual campers on this trip: an American lady, a Japanese man and a British man. We drove some four hours covering about 200 kilometers to Lake Nakuru, where we set up tents and then spent the afternoon gazing at the beauty of the lake. I captured the scenes with both my camera and my pen:

"On the edge of Lake Nakuru, 4.40 p.m.

---

[23] I paid 2350 Kenyan shillings instead of the published rate of 2900 shillings.

"Flamingoes. A pink sheet of them settling on Lake Nakuru. They provide such vivid contrast to the green of the grass and the blue of the water. From one end of the lake, they migrate to the other, forming a pink trail above the waters. Striking and elegant, they are a rare sight of wondrous beauty that is uniquely Nakuru.

"On the edge of Lake Nakuru, 5.00 p.m.

"The sun broke through the clouds and was the beauty of God's creation at its most brilliant display on Lake Nakuru. A whole mass of pink flamingoes decided to celebrate the exuberance of the sunshine by fluttering across the lake; they caused a momentary delight in us and we tried to capture this beautiful scene.

"At Baboon Cliff lookout point, 5.30 p.m.

"The whole lake comes into view. Like galaxies and stars in a universe, the pink conglomerates and clusters on Lake Nakuru are indeed an awe-inspiring sight."

Day 2 was spent mostly on the road. After having our breakfast (prepared by the cook) and dismantling the tents, we departed from Nakuru Lake and drove for more than two hours in the direction of Nairobi. The driver told us we would have lunch in a small town and then pick up four more campers – a young couple from Holland and a middle-aged couple from the United States -- before heading to Masai Mara. The journey after lunch was rough as we were driving on dirt tracks most of the way. By the time we reached the main gate of Masai Mara, it was already 6 p.m. and the sun was beginning to set. Seizing the last hour of daylight, we pitched our tents while the driver started a fire and the cook began preparing dinner for all of us. The meal was finally ready at 9.15 p.m. but for reasons unknown to me my stomach was gnawing in pain. It could be food poisoning, or pure motion sickness.

Anyway, the pain was so excruciating that I could not eat much; I simply rested.

When I came to consciousness on Day 3, daylight was already penetrating the thin layer of flysheet of the tent. I saw the driver washing himself in the stream next to our campsite and decided to join him. The water was cool and refreshing and seemed to have the magical quality to cleanse my digestive system. After the wash, I was ready to devour my breakfast and enjoy the two safari drives. The morning drive brought us into close contact with hyenas, wildebeests, elephants, and buffaloes; the one in the afternoon was less fruitful as we only came across a pair of cheetahs lying almost motionless in the open grassland. As we waited, they seemed to wish to reward our patience by standing up and licking each other. I captured that scene with my camera! That night, the entire group socialized around the campfire as our driver and cook taught us a Kenyan welcome song in Swahili.

The program on Day 4 was to me the most meaningful and rewarding. Our morning drive brought us to a river where we saw many hippopotamuses, all submerged in the muddy brown water save for their eyes which occasionally rose above the water level to peek at us. The driver then brought us to see a stone on which were written two letters, 'T' and 'K', representing Tanzania and Kenya respectively. In reality, Masai Mara National Reserve in Kenya and Serengati National Park in Tanzania, which occupies a much larger land area, are one, separated by an imaginary line that divides them.

As we moved on to look for lions, we passed by hundreds of wildebeests and a few zebras. The two species seemed to co-exist well with each other. When we finally found lions, we saw two lying passively under a big cactus tree licking their paws. Convinced that they would be lazing around for quite many hours, we decided to move on. Just then, the driver received information from another tour operator that a baby cheetah was spotted nearby, and he drove towards it, only to find it under the protection of its mother. This natural sense of protecting the young was also observed in a big elephant which shielded its baby when our vehicle drove towards them as we made our way to a Masai village.

A visit to Masai Mara without visiting the Masai cultural village would not be complete. On a plot of land about half the size of a standard football field, we saw many mud huts lined to form a rectangle measuring about 50 by 40 metres. Each mud hut measured approximately four by three by two metres and was separated from the next hut by about one meter. I entered one of the huts and was appalled by its condition. The doorway was narrow and low such that I had to bend my body to get in. Once inside, I could see a partitioned area about the size of two by one metre reserved for the family goats; turning left, I would see the only room, rectangular in shape, with a fireplace in the middle. On both sides of the fireplace were the sleeping areas for parents and children. Except for the doorway, the entire hut was in pitch darkness; light could penetrate only the sleeping quarters and the fireplace through some small holes measuring no bigger than two inches in diameter in the mud walls. After a short while, I could not bear the darkness and the smoke within and had to exit for fresh air. Little wonder why most of the Masai were found sitting or standing outside their huts or under a tree.

Apart from educating visitors, the cultural village also existed for commercial reasons. To enter the village, each visitor had to pay an entrance fee of 100 Kenyan shillings, after which he could take as many photographs as he liked. In the middle of the rectangle formed by the mud huts was a four-sided wooden fence on which were hung many colourful Masai handicrafts ranging from necklaces, headbands, earrings, and bangles. The Masai ladies were standing next to the handicrafts, gesturing to the visitors to examine them, and hopefully to buy them. These ladies were purveyors of Masai culture, wearing the colorful accessories as well as promoting them. I took many photographs of them, as well as the little children who wandered freely in this community. Last of all, I asked to have a photograph taken of me together with a Masai man who was holding a wooden club. It was an iconic shot of my time in Africa!

In the wee hours of Day 5, well before the sky brightened, I heard noises outside my tent. They did not sound like human footsteps; they were the heavy thumping sounds produced by animals. From the corner of my unzipped tent, I stole a glance and beheld the stripes of a herd of zebras. I heard their footsteps approaching our tents and then slowly fading away. Instantly, I took out my camera and fired a few shots at them from inside my tent, and the flash which accompanied each shot dazzled some of them as they hurried away. It dawned on me that I had witnessed real zebras crossing our campsite in the night! When daylight came, we had our last field breakfast and then bade farewell to Masai Mara. It was a long six-hour drive back to Nairobi, during which the driver kept persuading me to sell him my camera. I refused him repeatedly, citing sentimental value as the reason to keep the camera.

My last night in Nairobi was spent in the company of my fellow safari campers. Although we were staying in different hotels and guesthouses, we arranged to have dinner together to celebrate our friendship. Though we came from different countries, we connected well with one another and were bound by our common experience in Masai Mara. After our dinner, we adjourned to a café for beer and then to yet another for more beer, and only parted ways in the wee hours past midnight. Such was the strength of our bond of friendship.

On my last day in Nairobi, I had many hours on hand to get ready for the flight from Nairobi to Amsterdam which would depart at 11.45p.m. First, I went to Kenya Youth Hostel Association to check if my sister from Singapore had sent me any letter; I had given her instructions two months ago to write to me at this address if she would like to. True enough, a letter from my sister had just arrived. It was the first and last letter I received in Africa. In it, she updated me on her intention to delay her further studies, and the impending moving of house by my family in mid-September and gave me the new mailing address. Before she signed off, she left me with a piece of advice: 'Do not get yourself (*sic*) involved with cults.' This no doubt was a response to my frequent mention of God and praises accorded to Him in my previous letters and postcards. I understood the good intentions behind that advice.

Sincerely, my heart was filled with thanksgiving to God. At the end of two and a half months of wandering in Africa, there was so much I could give thanks for, and I shared these thanksgiving items with various individuals to whom I wrote: safe passage through five countries; sufficient funds to last the eleven weeks, including money to go on a camping safari; learning about the slave trade, and the works of missionaries like Dr David Livingstone and Dr Robert Laws to abolish slave trade and educate the locals; opportunities to ride on the Tazara train from Tanzania to Zambia, to live on a Zambian farm, to go on an overnight fishing trip on Lake Kariba with some commercial fishermen, to hike on Mulanje mountains, and to sail on the ferry Ilala on Lake Malawi; local people who had shown me kindness and hospitality in one way or another, including the Zambian police who interrogated me and sent me safely out of Zambia; and fellow solo backpackers who provided me with good company at unexpected moments.

With a heart full of thanksgiving, I departed Nairobi and returned to Loughborough via Amsterdam and London, ready to share the goodness of God with my friends.

CHAPTER 9

Flying to New York with a 'Mission'

Do not be yoked together with unbelievers. For what do righteousness and wickedness have in common? Or what fellowship can light have with darkness?

2 Corinthians 6:14

After two and a half months in Africa, I re-entered England with a reverse culture shock. What I used to take for granted as common occurrences repulsed me and struck me as shallow and superfluous: young couples displaying their affections publicly in acts of kissing, petting and necking; young girls in frivolous outfits puffing away at cigarettes and destroying their innocence and youth; and some overfed men shaved bald walking down the streets, displaying vulgar and revoltingly violent tattoos on their arms or chests. Such scenes paled in significance to the images of life and death that I had seen in Africa: the bony half-naked man on the beach of Dar es Salaam whose home was a shelter made of palm leaves; the mother who had to breastfeed two infants simultaneously on a long-distance bus journey to satisfy their hunger; and my young porter who had to brave the cold of the Mulanje mountains with no shoes and no windbreaker. I needed time to reconcile the polarity of superfluity and poverty on this planet.

Was I glad for a week of settling down in Loughborough before my final year commenced in early October 1988. There were plenty of immediate tasks to be accomplished; I was moving into a rented house together with three other students, two from Singapore and one from Sweden, and had to spend time getting to know them and our landlady. In a postcard dated 10th October 1988, I informed my sister that I had many pre-occupations on my mind then: handing over the responsibilities of running the Singapore Society in my university to the newly-elected committee, trying to arrange a cheap flight home to Singapore during the Christmas vacation, arranging the photographs taken in Africa and sending some of them to various individuals in different African countries, and settling down to serious reading and studying. Never in my imagination then did I expect that above all this, I was to be given a 'mission' that would consume a lot of my time and emotional energy, and ultimately test my faith in the God I had grown to know and love.

The mission had to do with the progress and continuation of my relationship with a girl, known, for reason of confidentiality, as K. After our junior college days, we went our separate ways: K to university and I to the army. However, we kept in touch with each other through postcards, greeting cards and letters. Of the many friends that I corresponded with on a regular basis, K was one of the few I connected with on a more intimate and deeper level, one with whom I could openly share my dreams and aspirations with. Call it 'human chemistry', call it 'the same wavelength', we touched each other's heart in our regular sharing of ourselves and our values, but it was always from a physical distance. And this physical distance was breached four years later in late December 1988 when I flew from London to New York to meet her. I was in New York with a mission.

The meeting was unplanned but arose out of my growing faith in God and her desire to find out more about my faith. In early 1987, after my first solo trip to Germany, I received a card from K with these words printed on it: "You've given me a lot to smile about!" and wished me a 'Happy Valentine's Day' and that I might 'fall in love with someone.' A year later, in early 1988, I received another card from K, but this time, it came from the United States where she had gone to pursue a master's degree. The card came with these printed words: "Happy Valentine's Day from the most ardent of your admirers" and she added, "I hope you find someone to love, not to mention the fact that everyone already loves you!"

However, by the middle of the year, she wrote with a pensive tone: "... it's difficult to converse with you, knowing that now you have found light... I understand your strong encouragement for me to seek Christ. I hope you are not too disappointed that I haven't made much effort in doing so. I hope you understand." Then in late August, she wrote again, in response to a letter I sent her from Harare in Zimbabwe, the contents of which eluded me; she wrote, "I hope you understand and still love me; love me as a person and not because I am your sister in God... I am a Buddhist" and ended the letter by requesting that we meet in person at the end of the year after her graduation so that I could enlighten her on the many questions that she had concerning religion in general and Christianity in particular. Her earnest request resulted in our meeting in late December 1988 in New York.

In retrospect, as I examined the chronology of this series of events culminating in her request for us to meet, I marveled at God's perfect timing and provision. K's letter written in late August of 1988 reached me in Loughborough only upon my return from Africa in late September. By then, God had already given me very good reasons why I should not allow my relationship with K to continue to grow in intimacy. After sending K a letter from Harare, I found myself spending the next five days in Kariba where, by divine appointment, I picked up a four-page pamphlet entitled '*Why You Shouldn't Marry Or Date An Unbeliever*'. Needless to say, given the many hours of waiting for transport in Africa and being by myself most of the time, I devoured the content, scrutinized it and reflected on the issues surfaced, such as how my relationship with God and with my future spouse would be affected if I married a non-believer, and how raising children would be a source of conflict given the vast differences in our value systems. I was convinced that it was not a path I should take.

My mind was firm about my course of action in New York, but my spirit was weak in executing it. In the first two days of our togetherness, I found it difficult to broach the subject of being 'unequally yoked with unbelievers'[24].

---

24   This phrase, taken from 2 Corinthians 16:14, refers to intimate relationships with unbelievers. In this context, it refers to Christians marrying unbelievers.

We were glad to see each other after so many years and engaged in small talk to update each other on our personal lives; neither of us had the courage to go straight to the point. Internally, I struggled and cried out to God to help me, as reflected in my diary entry in the early morning of the third day:

> "I cried. I woke up and thought and cried and cried. My tears, warm and surging, flowed ceaselessly. This very knot is beyond me and my ability to untie. I know not how to act: to love one whom I must not love, or to unlove one whom I seem eternally bound to love? My mind, like a floating object in a turbulent sea, tossed, turned, washed up and down, was the instigator of this human conflict. But it too was the tranquilizer that assuaged my pain when it persisted against all odds to dwell on high and sing praises to Him…"

By the end of that same day, incidentally a rainy day, I thanked God for the great outpouring from my heart, as recorded in my diary:

> "Infinitely, infinitely, O God, thou reign forever. Love so free, faith so strong, thou has strengthened me beyond measure, and given me the desire of my heart without sinning against thee. Wonderful Lord, my Father, all praise I give to thee for this great outpouring of truth in the

café, that light and darkness have nothing
in common and cannot have true union.
How sweet were the words that came out
of my mouth and how delicately thou hast
prepared her heart to accept this truth.
The utterance of truth has every power
and dominion over falsehood and deceit.
Thy truth, O Lord, sets us free, free from
the bondage of destructible human love."

The releasing of the truth somehow brought us together in a more certain and dignified manner. We laid down some ground rules with regard to physical intimacy, and our bond of friendship was seemingly further strengthened.

The human heart, however, has its distinctive mysteries. It yearns to touch and to be touched, to love and to be loved; yet it invariably at times chooses to withdraw, to distance and to spite the object of love. Remaining in a state of flux between attraction and repulsion, between reason and passion, my heart rioted rigorously within my soul in the next few days. I continued reading the Bible daily but K did not show interest in it; I also read Joyce Huggett's book, *Just Good Friends?: Growing in Relationships,* which I brought along with me. As I read, I began to question if I was being selfish in our act of physical togetherness, causing her unseen harm. Such thoughts troubled me, and I resolved to discuss this question of physical intimacy with K. Somehow, my question, raised from a Christian perspective, angered her and she withdrew herself from me, causing me to feel the alienation and the chasm in our ways of thinking.

For the entire duration of twelve days that I spent in New York, we did not travel outside of the city. We simply spent time in the house belonging to K's friend's aunt, going out for movies, dinner, occasional shopping and strolling in Central Park. It was strictly speaking not my preferred way of travelling, which should encompass long distance transport, some degree of uncertainty and surprises, and frequent changes in scenery and landscape, like the one I just completed in Africa a few months ago. However, this trip to New York was intense and challenging in an emotional sense. I was constantly drawn into a physical relationship with K since we could not connect on a spiritual level, with the word of God acting as my chaperon. In a sense, the trip marked a milestone in my spiritual journey when I was able to take a stand to obey and honor God's word. On the flip side, it also allowed me to see my own sinfulness and need for God's holiness.

God was with me throughout my intense struggle within me, although at times I felt far from Him. On the second last day of my time in New York, He spoke through two verses from the Bible during my morning devotional time: "Blessed are they who keep his statues and seek him with all their heart" (Psalm 119:2) and "Rend your heart and not your garments. Return to the Lord your God, for he is gracious and compassionate, slow to anger and abounding in love, and he relents from sending calamity" (Joel 2:13). He was asking me to seek Him and His way, and not to give my heart away to another.

In the evening that day, God spoke again through a most unexpected way. After watching a movie, K and I went to separate restrooms for the two different genders. When I came out from the male restroom, I waited a long time for her to appear, but she was nowhere to be seen. In my desperation, I told God I was willing to let her go if only He would help us find each other. Soon after my silent prayer, K walked towards me. According to her, she had waited for me for some minutes and then, thinking that I might have walked further ahead, she went in search for me. How this entire episode could be logically pieced together I had no idea because I did not dally in the washroom; one thing was sure, God's hand was in it and He was reminding me to let go of K, emotionally, in my heart.

A week after my return to Loughborough, I received a letter written over two separate days from K. In it, she expressed her feelings of missing me, and apologized for causing me "so much trouble, so much pain," and updated me on her change of plans for flying home. There was no mention of God. In my heart, I asked God: "O God, have I failed you in the 'mission' you entrusted to me? Have I engaged her sufficiently in conversations about God? Or have I allowed our human emotions to hold sway over our physical relationship?"

In my lengthy reply to her letter, I tried to point her to God's love lived out in a practical human way:

> "Your first letters of the year 1989 arrived this morning. I read them in bed – and how did I feel? I was glad to hear from you, to be reassured that you're still out there, and I maintaining some contact with you. I also felt a pleasant strain, that my emotion was stretched and held in an unresolved tension, reaching out and held suspended on the other end

by you and your missing me...the short spell of 12 days with you had taught me a great deal about love – which is God and originates from God. The joy and trauma of our being together had opened up a new horizon, a new perspective of deeper understanding of His love. And to emulate it and live up to it is no mean measure of effort and will. This love is not self-centered but focuses on the ones loved, so that the best is intended for those on the receiving end, regardless of their goodness or vileness.

"This is how God showed his love among us: He sent his one and only Son into the world that we might live through him. This is love: not that we loved God, but that he loved us and sent his Son as an atoning sacrifice for our sins. Dear friends, since God so loved us, we also ought to love one another (1 John 4:9-11).

"My command is this: Love each other as I have loved you. Greater love has no one than this: to lay down one's life for one's friends (John 15:12-13)."

It was interesting that K ended her letter with a request: "I should begin work soon. Pray for me now, if you will." I did not let this request slip in my reply and attached a prayer of blessing for her future: "As you travel through life, may you always have happiness, hope, success, friends and faith… to make each day better from this day forth."

Truth be told that it was not easy for me to let go of K entirely in my emotions. In the deepest recesses of my mind, I was still harboring a faint hope that she might turn to God and receive His love, so that both of us could connect also on a spiritual plane. While waiting impatiently for her to reply my letter dated 15th Jan 1989, I wrote her a poem on 4th Feb, which in essence was an invitation for her to join me in the Christian faith:

"Do You Want to Fly with Me?

"I am a seagull, lonesome and wild,
The world in all its immensity is my home,
I fly, high, so high I could reach the sky,
And glide in joyous hope and spirit free.
Lo! Beneath me, the world is my eye.

I would fly to yonder pasture green
To feast on life's treasure that gleam
The beauty and majesty of His heavenly
That breeds all creatures big and small.
Lo! Before me, the world is my mind.

I would go travelling down the valley
Across the sea, to the hills and dales,
Meeting fellow gulls, sharing their stories,
Being one of them, for once, for eternity.
Lo! Inside me, the world is my life.

But on one such journey would I meet
A charming gull in solitary flight,

Her motion seems one with the wind,
But her spirit is not altogether free.
'Hey! My dear friend, this is the right way!'

Do you want to fly with me?
Or have you no will enough, no wings?"

As I browsed through my diary from January to May of 1989, I noted instances when my faith was weak and my spirit wrestled with God, but He was ever so patient with me, encouraging me to submit to His higher and better will:

"26th Jan 1989. Reaffirmed my faith, re-dedicated my complete self to God, to walk in the Spirit."

"27th Feb 1989. Dreamt such vivid and poignant dreams about K... I was embracing her from behind, and she drew me closer... I awoke feeling the need to reach her, and the distance in between."

"21st Mar 1989. Today was one such day when K came to mind, so vividly, so beautifully, so inevitably sadly. I thought and recalled the days spent in New York with her; I swallowed the words of God; I prayed. And God spoke through Jeremiah 15:18-20:

"18 Why is my pain unending
and my wound grievous and incurable?
You are to me like a deceptive brook, like a spring that fails.

19 Therefore this is what the Lord says:
'If you repent, I will restore you that you may serve me;

if you utter worthy, not worthless, words, you will be
my spokesman.
Let this people turn to you, but you must not turn
to them.
20 I will make you a wall to this people, a fortified
wall of bronze;
they will fight against you but will not overcome you,
for I am with you to rescue and save you,' declares
the Lord."

Through this passage from the book of Jeremiah,
God was addressing the unending pain in my heart and
asking me to repent of my persistent clinging onto K.
Only when I did that would He restore me and use me
as His spokesperson to the people of the world—those
who do not know God. And surely it was no coincidence
that on 3rd April 1989, I should receive a letter from Sue,
one of the two lady missionaries with whom I went to
Java, Indonesia, in the summer of 1987. In the letter,
Sue encouraged me to guard myself against the wayward
temptations of this world, of intellect, beauty and art, and
she signed off with this verse: 'Seek first his kingdom and
his righteousness, and all others will be added onto you
(Matthew 6:33).'

The following day, God continued to speak to me
through a word given to me in my dream, as recorded in
my diary:

"4th April 1989. Woke up remembering the word
'heifer'. Must be from the Lord. The word looked strange
and yet I was sure of its spelling. The dictionary says of
'heifer': a young cow that has not yet had a calf. What
could it possibly mean for me? A burnt offering? I spent

the whole day reading Elizabeth-Ann Horsford's *Complete As One.*[25]Came across a passage about living for Christ, presenting our bodies as a living sacrifice for God. That's it – a heifer is a living sacrifice.

"Knelt and prayed as the total discipline of abiding in Christ frightened me. Was God calling me into a life of celibacy? Was He preparing me for it? I confessed to Him my anxiety and my fear. Then methought a small inner voice said, 'Get up and walk five steps.' I did, though it sounded silly. That brought me before the glass window. I looked out and began to ask Him, 'What now?' And as I pressed my forehead and my nose against the glass pane, a gust suddenly shook the glass violently. I could not understand it…"

"5th April 1989. I knew it must be it. The Lord's voice telling me gently, 'The wind, the wind, I was in that wind.' I woke up suddenly and rejoiced."

"21st May 1989. Read '*Why You Shouldn't Marry Or Date An Unbeliever*', the pamphlet I picked up from Kariba, again. Gave myself unreservedly to the Lord."

For reasons unknown to me, I never received any more letters from K after her first letters in January 1989. Was she acting of her own volition or was she responding to a piece of advice, or even a rule imposed on her? I had no way of finding out, nor was it necessary for me to ascertain the reasons. From what happened on the second last day in New York, and my subsequent hearing from God, it was clear that He wanted me to let go of K, to disentangle myself emotionally from this relationship. But

---

[25] A Christian book which advocates that singleness can also be completeness if the life is lived with and for God.

I was unwilling to let her go completely, and God had to deal with my disobedience and stubbornness before He could bless me with a Christian life partner.

In the Bible, there is a famous story about Abraham sacrificing his son Isaac (Genesis 22). The story begins with these words: 'God tested Abraham'. God asked Abraham to sacrifice his only beloved son Isaac as a burnt offering on one of the mountains in the region of Moriah. Abraham obeyed God and went on a long journey; on the third day, he saw the mountain. Then, he gave instructions to his servants to remain with the donkey while he and his son Isaac went up the mountain to 'worship' God. I would like to believe that Abraham struggled intensely in his heart as he went on the three-day journey; however, eventually he decided to worship God by being obedient to Him, even if that meant sacrificing his only beloved son, Isaac. And Abraham probably left his servants behind because he did not want them to stop him from worshipping God on the mountain—sacrificing his son.

God sent me on a mission to New York to make it known to K that light and darkness cannot co-exist; I obeyed and went. But God also wanted me to release K emotionally from my heart; I was less willing to do so and struggled intensely in my inmost being. Unlike Abraham who was single-minded in executing God's instructions and did not allow any human agents to stop him from worshipping God – sacrificing his son, I employed the art of poetry[26] to lure K into a spiritual journey with me when this was not part of God's instructions. In the story, Abraham passed the test of faith; in my case, I tested the patience of God by taking a long time to release K from

---

[26]   See the poem "*Do You Want to Fly with Me?*"

my heart. When I eventually did, God brought a Christian girl into my life to 'fly with me', and after much seeking of the Lord's will, we were united in matrimony in 1994.

To love God is to submit whole-heartedly to Him, without any reservation.

CHAPTER 10

Trekking in the Kelabit Highlands

If I rise on the wings of the dawn, if I settle on the far side of the sea, even there your hand will guide me, your right hand will hold me fast.

Psalm 139: 9-10

The months after my return from New York were filled with intense emotional struggle and surrender. By God's grace, I managed to summon all the concentration I needed to complete every assignment before my final examinations in June. In a letter dated 11th May 1989 to Aunt Eunice, a devout Catholic, I wrote:

> "Indeed, we have much to rejoice in the Lord. Every new day is a gift, a time to appreciate small little things we have and can do. And when we delight in Him and His wonderful creation on Earth, there's

peace in our mind and joy in our heart,
so pure and overflowing it can hardly
be expressed adequately and accurately...
Now I have exactly one month to revise
for my finals which will take place in
the last three weeks of June. There's no
unnecessary pressure; there's only faith in
Him and His goodness as I confront the
coming weeks. One must be wary though
to see that one is always putting God
before all else, 'to seek first His kingdom
and His righteousness' Matthew 6:33."

With God's help, the finals came and went very
smoothly. Soon after my finals, I went on a two-week
Western Europe tour with my mother and my sister,
who flew from Singapore, and my sister's fiancé, who
flew from Scotland after completing his studies there.
We booked a Trafalgar tour departing from London and
visited Belgium, Germany, Austria, Italy, Switzerland and
France. For me, it was a time to bond with my mother
and my sister, and to get to know my future brother-
in-law better; for my mother, it was a celebration to see
her son complete his university degree; and for my sister
and her fiancé, it was a time to be re-united after the
latter's two-year studies in Scotland. All in all, we had a
relaxing time cruising and sightseeing in Europe, being
completely detached from the tragedy and suffering that
was happening in Beijing, China.

Upon my return to Singapore, I received an
impassioned letter (re-directed from Loughborough) from
Patrizia, one of the music students I met in Bologna,
Italy a year ago. In her letter, she sent me her 'deep love

in Christ' and her 'solidarity for what's happened and is still happening to your people in China,' referring to the Tiananmen massacre that took place in Beijing on 4th June that year. She expressed her 'rage, deep pain and sorrow' as well as her 'great admiration for all those young people still able to die for an ideal' and decried the superficial preoccupations of the Italians with money, career and women. Her polemic against the casual indifference of the Europeans towards this catastrophic event in China really put me to shame; through her letter, I identified myself as one of those who did not respond strongly to and condemn the atrocities committed in China; in fact, I was luxuriating in the warm sunshine of a busy summer in Europe. At the close of her letter, she offered her strong solidarity and prayer for me and the Chinese people. I was touched beyond words.

In my reply to Patrizia, apart from telling her that Singapore and China are two different countries quite far apart in geographical distance, I saluted her for her close identification with the suffering of the Chinese and concurred with her view on the cold collective response of European countries. I wrote:

> "… your concern for the Chinese students in China really touched me, and in a way put shame to my casual indifference. For this, you are more than a friend – a warrior, a compassionate helper, a disciple of Christ! … You mentioned the collective indifference and coldness of the European society in response to this crisis… I must say that the world at large has along with the growth of material wealth and

worldly affluence become uncaring and more self-centered. This attitude is by no means exclusively a European illness, if one can call it such. The world will 'keep on failing and falling' so long as man has not reconciled himself with God, that is, not known the love of Christ. We know full well that since Adam and Eve, nobody is born without sin. And sin leads to death, physical and spiritual death, and in the case of China, death of humanity... May your prayers keep reaching out to the Chinese students, and may the Lord keep you and bless you."

Though the reporting of the Tiananmen incident in the British newspapers pained me in the early part of June, the massacre seemed far away once I was back in Singapore in mid-July. I spent my time reconnecting with my family and some former classmates, participating in an Under-23 inter-club rugby competition, and reading a number of books. In addition, I made a trip to the Kelabit Highlands in Borneo. This was the result of reading about an Englishman's travels in Borneo in a book called *A Stroll Through Borneo*. I was drawn by the remoteness of the highlands and the diversity of the ethnic tribes found in Sarawak. To me, it was like taking a journey back to nature where people lived in harmony with their surroundings and their way of life was unspoiled by the pervasive use of technology. After my travels in Africa a summer ago, I longed to experience life in its simpler and more primitive form. And such a way of life can be found in the rural areas of Sarawak, not too far from Singapore!

The journey from Singapore to the Kelabit Highlands was a long drawn-out one requiring several stops. First, a flight from Johor Bahru[27] to Kuching, the capital of Sarawak; then a five-hour boat trip from Kuching to Sibu; followed by an eight-hour bus journey from Sibu to Miri; and finally, a short flight from Miri to Bario, the centre of the Kelabit Highlands. The entire journey took a few days. Along the way, I could see the hand of God protecting me. For instance, on arrival at the Methodist Guest House in Sibu by taxi, the driver drove off before I had unloaded my luggage. Upon realizing this, I wasted no time and dashed down the road in the merciless rain, praying desperately as I ran, and at the same time, thinking what I would do if I failed to locate the taxi. I must have run about 200 meters or so when the taxi suddenly stopped, and as the driver wound down the window, I thanked God that it was the right taxi. Phew! What a great relief it was to me!

The flight from Miri to Bario was one of the highlights of the entire trip. As the landing strip in Bario was an open field then[28], only small aircrafts could land on it. On rainy days, the field would be wet or even flooded, and no plane could land or take off from it. Thus, flying into and out of Bario was highly dependent on the unpredictable highland weather. I was fortunate to be able to fly into Bario in a Twin Otter operated by Malaysian Airline System (MAS) on a clear day on 26th August 1989. The small aircraft had a total capacity of 19 seats, excluding the two seats at the cockpit for the pilot and co-pilot. There

---

[27] I flew from Johor Bahru because it was and still is significantly cheaper than flying from Singapore.

[28] Bario now has an all-weather modern tarmac runway.

were altogether eleven passengers that day, and each of us and our luggage had to be weighed so that the total load of the aircraft could be calculated. In a way, such meticulous calculations gave passengers a sense of security, that safety was not compromised.

Taking the 50-minute flight in a Twin Otter was an experience of a lifetime. Due to the proximity of the aircraft engine and its propellers to the cabin, it was extremely noisy throughout the flight. However, the magnificent aerial view of the lush tropical jungle bisected by the mighty serpentine Baram River more than made up for the inconvenience. For the first time since lower secondary Geography days, I saw oxbow lakes from a vantage point up in a plane. Above the lush green of the forest and the meandering river and its tributaries, pockets of clouds floated and drifted by; sometimes thick, sometimes thin, the passing clouds gave me the sensation that the plane I was in just floated alongside them effortlessly, suspended in air without the propulsion of an engine. In this way, the plane seemingly drifted above valleys and hills towards the Kelabit Highlands.

Sitting on an elevation of 1000 meters above sea level, the Bario plain appeared quite suddenly in the midst of a multitude of hills. In no time, the pilot successfully landed the aircraft on the airfield and some ground staff walked towards it to unload the luggage. I was fortunate to have met a West Malaysian, Raja, who was then teaching in a secondary school in Brunei, on the same flight. As both of us had the intention to trek in the Kelabit Highlands, we decided to embark on this adventure together. But first, we had to hire a local guide. After some consultation with the soldiers stationed at Bario, a rough sketch of the route covering a few villages around Bario and crossing the border into Kalimantan in Indonesia was suggested. All in all, the entire trek would take four days. With that knowledge, we went to the MAS office to reserve two seats for our outward- bound flight for 30th August, flying from Bario to Marudi, with no promise of seats for the final leg from Marudi to Miri.

Having settled our return flights and hired a guide, Yusop, we went to purchase some ration for the four-day journey. It was then that we discovered that all the food items were more expensive compared to those in bigger cities like Kuching and Miri. This was inevitable, though, since everything had to be flown in from bigger cities. To equip us for the trek, the soldiers lent us mesh tins and water bottles and even gave us salt and solid fuel; in addition, they also agreed to safe-keep some of our belongings which really helped to lighten our load. One of the soldiers even brought us to the police station where the chief typed a permit for us to cross the border into Kalimantan. In the process of preparation, we forgot to have lunch but set off immediately when the paperwork was completed. The prospect of meeting the Kelabit people in the villages excited us so much that all trivial matters were relegated to the back of our minds. Fortunately, we did not forget to fill our water bottles.

The hike from Bario to Pa Lungan, our first stopover, was a fairly manageable one which took us slightly more than three and a half hours inclusive of small breaks. Our guide Yusop was a lean and diminutive man with strong arms and legs. Though he measured only 1.3 meters in height, he was a tanned and seasoned man used to the terrain and usually walked briskly ahead of Raja and me. Walking out of Bario, we passed by many paddy fields which soon gave way to lalang (a coarse, weedy grass), ferns and tropical rainforests with occasional sightings of wild orchids and vibrant rhododendron bushes. At some point, it reminded me of my army training in the jungles of Brunei, only this time I was wearing a T-shirt and a pair of colorful shorts with no rifle slinging across my shoulder. As we neared the village of Pa Lungan, we had to cross a suspended wooden bridge that looked like a much simpler version of the Golden Gate Bridge of San Francisco. Here, Raja and I took turns to take a photograph with Yusop.

Upon our arrival at Pa Lungan, Yusop brought us to meet the village chief. He welcomed us through his simple gestures of handshake. With him was a couple from Britain and they were pleased to meet other visitors who could speak English. Raja's ability to speak both English and Bahasa Melayu was a great asset. Through him, some of the questions we had about life in a longhouse were answered by the chief, through whom we learned a great deal about the culture of the Kelabit people. For instance, having stretched earlopes was considered a form of beauty by the Kelabit people in the past but this was increasingly seen by the younger generations as being old-fashioned. Indeed, those with extended earlopes whom we saw at the Bario airstrip in the morning were the elderly in their fifties and sixties.

After spending some time with the village chief, Yusop brought us to his relatives' longhouse in Pa Lungan where we were to spend the night. We were greeted by a male head of the family and four other women, all without extended earlopes. How the four women were related to one another and to the man I had no idea and did not have the language to make enquiries. While Raja conversed with the family head in Bahasa Melayu, I sat next to him observing his facial expressions, benefiting occasionally from Raja's translation. The four ladies in the meantime prepared and cooked dinner over a natural fire whose smoke dried the firewood placed a meter or more above it. In between, Yusop, Raja and I took turns to shower. Was the water cold in the evening!

Four pairs of seasoned hands soon put together a Kelabit dinner for the eight of us. There were six dishes comprising dried fish, wild Kelabit spinach and other highland vegetables whose names eluded me, and a liberal serving of sticky Bario rice, all laid out on a straw mat around which we sat. As there was no electricity in this village, three small gas lamps were placed at different corners of the mat. Not having had lunch earlier in the day, and having trekked for more than three hours, we were naturally famished. After the Christian head of the family had given thanks for the food, we eagerly helped ourselves to the nourishment. I found the rice fragrant and the dishes appetizing -- a satisfying dinner that concluded our first day of trekking.

I was awoken by the sound of a gong at five o'clock in the morning when the sky was still pitch dark. As I tossed in my sleeping bag, I thought this village a very organized and militant one with a morning call for all; still, I knew that the call was not for me, a visitor, and went back to sleep. Later at breakfast time, I learned that the gong was their daily morning call for the Christian community to arise for morning prayers. What solid discipline! The Christians in Pa Lungan have much to teach other Christian communities all over the world! I wonder how many Christians in big cities would be committed to attend prayer meetings at such an unearthly hour.

After breakfast, we set off at about 8.20 a.m. for Pa Rupai, a village just across the Sarawak-Kalimantan border. We were joined by John, an Englishman teaching in Brunei, who was heading the same way. The route was longer and much more energy-sapping compared to the day before; as a result of the heavy rain the night before, the paths were slippery and muddy, and the streams were swollen. Along the way, we had to negotiate steep slopes which were arduous to ascend and descend. On many occasions, we had to wade through ankle-deep and knee-deep streams, which made our shoes and socks heavy. But what proved more challenging was to spot the leeches that had found their way into our shoes and underneath our socks to suck our blood. Every now and then, one of us would stop walking to remove these persistent pests from our legs but our occasional searches were never foolproof: some leeches were so firmly embedded inside our shoes that we could not find them till we completely removed our shoes.

To add to the misery of the journey, it started to rain again at about 4 p.m. At one stage, Yusop and John, being fitter, went so far ahead that Raja and I lost track of their backs. We broke contact and no amount of shouting was of use; the pelting rain was so noisy it drowned out our voices. Then, Raja and I decided to backtrack some distance as we were not sure if we had deviated from the route. At this point, I fell into a prayerful mood to seek the Lord's mercy and help. Somehow, after some deliberation, we decided to push straight on. A short distance further up, we heard Yusop shouting for us, and a sense of relief immediately came over us. In my heart, I was filled with gratitude that even in such a rural and remote surrounding, God heard and answered my prayer.

The four of us walked on for another hour or so before paddy fields came into sight. The fields were a welcoming sight as it meant that a village was nearby. Crossing many man-made bridges and low wooden fences, we finally arrived at Pa Rupai. Yusop brought us to a longhouse where we greeted the head of the family. We were glad that the long and wet day of trekking had come to an end, but first, we had to deal with the merciless leeches. As I removed my shoes, I could see patches of blood stains on my socks, and many leeches were still clinging onto my skin and sucking my blood. After pulling the leeches out in a careful manner, and ensuring that our legs were free from them, we went to the nearby river for an ablution. The water not only cleansed our wounds but also provided the much-needed therapeutic effect of relaxing our tense muscles. Back in the longhouse, we sat near the fireplace to warm ourselves and to wait patiently for our dinner.

There was no record in my diary of what was served at dinner at Pa Rupai. Perhaps it was already dark by then and the longhouse was dimly lit by the gas lamps placed around it, and I was less than observant after a day's walk and too tired after dinner to write. However, it was reasonable to assume that the food was most satisfying and appreciated by all of us after our long and exhausting trek to the village. At about 10 p.m. we retired to our sleeping bags. In my semi-conscious state, I could still hear the indigenous people chatting, almost whispering, but it did not last for long.

I came to consciousness in the morning and heard hurrying footsteps in the longhouse. The residents were already up and preparing for the day's work. Women were seen preparing breakfast and packing rice in banana leaves (to be brought to the paddy fields for lunch) while men were getting the equipment ready to go out to the fields. After our breakfast, we spent some time taking photos with the three-generational family in the roomy longhouse. Unlike the longhouse in Pa Lungan, this one was better furnished with a small table and some chairs at one corner of the longhouse, and even glass windowpanes.

We set off at 8.20 a.m. with renewed energy for our third day of trekking. We passed by one paddy field after another and finally came to a split point where Yusop asked both Raja and me to wait while he showed John the track leading to Ba Kelalan. When Yusop returned, we continued our trek towards Long Medan, only a few kilometers from Pa Rupai. He brought us to his parents' house to rest while he went to look for three motorcycles to take us to Long Bawan, the main town where we needed to register ourselves with the local police. His advice was that we should arrive at Long Bawan in a more official way, failing which some corrupt immigration officials might make it difficult for us to register our names. We duly took his advice and mounted the three motorcycles.

The ride on a motorcycle from Long Medan to Long Bawan was really an experience by itself. Passing through narrow footpaths, muddy lanes, inclined slopes, suspension bridges and scenic paddy fields, and being constantly jerked up and down, we arrived at Long Bawan, a relatively big town, within half an hour. Our first stop was the immigration office where we registered ourselves and paid five Malaysian ringgits each as immigration charges. The officer was friendly towards us and even agreed to have a photograph taken together with me. After that, at our request, Yusop brought us to visit a school in town and we interacted briefly with the staff who were hospitable and did not mind our informal attire. Though their staff room was small, I noted that it was clean and tidy, and had electricity supply.

After having some food for lunch and replenishing ourselves with fresh supplies of sugar, tea leaves and sardine to be given as gifts for our host family at the end of the day, we pressed on towards our destination, Lembudud. The scenery along the way was not as interesting as that between Long Medan and Long Bawan. It was just one dirt track after another, a monotonous landscape. Then the drizzle turned into rain as the hours went by. By six in the evening, the sky was already in semi–darkness and our destination was still not within sight. We therefore quickened our pace, and only made it to Lembudud at a quarter to seven. Yusop quickly located the village chief's longhouse and we were cordially invited to be his guests for the evening. For dinner that day, we had rice and three simple dishes which we ate with thanksgiving; outside the longhouse, it was pouring heavily.

The rain must have stopped before the break of a new day. After breakfast and spending some time taking photographs with our host family, we set off at about 8.35 a.m. for our final destination, Bario. According to the chief, it would be a six-hour walk, but in reality we took much longer than that. One possible reason could be that after two and a half days of trekking, we were feeling the strain on our bodies. Nevertheless, we were grateful for his advice on combating the attack of leeches: he gave us bars of soap to rub on our socks, and this method proved rather effective. On the way, though we forded many streams, we had fewer leech assaults compared to the second day.

The route between Bario and Lembudud must be a common thoroughfare. On the way, we met many trekkers and locals heading in both directions. The latter gave us a rough idea of the walking speed of the Kelabit natives. If we were walking in the same direction, within two or three minutes, we would have lost complete trace of them. Some of them wore only shoes without socks; a girl even went barefooted. Despite us wearing better shoes, we could not keep pace with them and had to go at our own speed. Thus, we learned to adjust our expectations whenever the locals gave us a rough estimate of the time needed to cover a certain distance; often, we had to add another 50 percent to their estimation of time needed to cover a distance, and more if the conditions of the paths were muddy.

Notwithstanding our slower pace, we had complete trust in our guide Yusop to lead us to Bario by the end of the day. We plodded on through the muddy jungle paths, being careful not to slip as far as we could help it. But it was not always possible. Once, we came across another guide heading in the opposite direction. Noticing that we were walking without any aid, he very kindly offered each of us a thin but sturdy walking stick, which helped us gain more balance when we walked. We were much encouraged by his kind gesture and persevered. As the sun was about to set at 6.30p.m., we finally caught sight of our destination. Walking into Bario, my heart was filled with thanksgiving to God for His wonderful provision and protection along the way.

Upon arriving in Bario, we went straight to the immigration office to inform them of our return. After some food, we checked into a guesthouse, showered and warmed ourselves near the fireplace. It had been one long and tiring day—we walked ten hours! More than that, the four-day trek was a good introduction to the culture of the Kelabit Highlands—the food, the longhouses, the way of life which embraced nature wholeheartedly yet did not reject the use of technology such as electricity and motor-bicycles altogether. The best part of the Kelabit culture was the hospitality and willingness of the people to share their culture with the outside world.

The next day started with promise and expectation. It was a clear morning and the small aircraft was expected to land in Bario. After breakfast, Raja and I went to the army tent to return the mesh tins and water bottles that we had borrowed, and to collect the belongings that we had deposited with them. However, shortly after we had been served drinks, it began to rain, heavier and heavier. Later, at about 10 a.m., a check with the MAS office confirmed that the morning flight had been cancelled, and on top of that, no chartered flights would take place since all planes would be used to transport VIPs and the props needed for the Malaysia National Day celebration in Kapit, Sarawak.

Determined to make the best of the situation, Raja and I decided to walk around Bario to acquaint ourselves with this gem which is the heart of the Kelabit Highlands. We passed by paddy fields and saw many buffaloes being used to pull carts loaded with goods. Here and there, the Kelabit people were at work— women carrying baskets on their backs and men walking their buffaloes to or from the paddy fields. When we came across the elderly with long earlobes, we asked for permission to be photographed with them, and out of their friendliness, they willingly consented. Truly, the locals lived up to their reputation as a hospitable people; their friendliness proved that Bario is indeed 'the land of a hundred handshakes'.

The name 'Bario' in the Kelabit language means 'wind'. As Raja and I walked towards Bario Primary

School, we were enchanted by the music that floated in the wind. Gathered in the school hall were about 80 or more students sitting on wooden benches, all brimming and radiant, eagerly rehearsing their presentation of a song for Malaysia's National Day the next day. The older girls were playing beautiful music on their bamboo flutes, with the accompaniment of bamboo bass provided by the older boys who were playing on blowpipe-like bamboo instruments. The younger ones sat by the side and sang. Their voices were loud and in unison, and they had no qualms about singing in the presence of foreigners like Raja and me. I was impressed by their attentiveness and engagement in the piece of music; I was also charmed by the innocent and carefree look on their faces, as well as the seriousness with which the teacher conducted the rehearsal. Together, they formed the choir and the bamboo band of Bario, rendering music of the purest kind in the Kelabit Highlands. Raja and I were indeed privileged to be the only audience of that divine piece of music.

Apart from the school, we also experienced the hospitality of Bario through our interaction with the staff of MAS. In the process of arranging for a flight to take us out of Bario, we spoke to Rose, the manageress, and two ladies who shared much of the Kelabit culture with us. Out of her desire to give us a glimpse of her culture, Rose invited us to her longhouse for dinner that evening, which we gladly accepted. The visit would afford us a basis for comparison between the longhouses in Bario, the centre of the Kelabit highlands, and the ones we visited in the interior of the highlands.

On arrival at Rose's house, we met her father, an elderly gentleman with long earlobes on which were hung two gold rings, and her immediate family who had stopped the practice of elongating their earlobes. Unlike the longhouses that we visited along the trek, in Rose' longhouse we dined around a long table and sat on individual chairs with back supports. The food was sumptuous; we had meat and vegetable dishes along with the tasty Bario rice. During the meal, we were repeatedly asked to eat more, to finish the rice in our bowl, lest the rain would not stop and consequently we would not be able to fly out of Bario. After dinner, we relaxed around the fireplace and had a pleasant conversation about the changing landscape of Bario and the mindset of its people. It was not till past 10 p.m. that we thanked our hostess and departed from the longhouse, walking with utmost caution back to our guesthouse lest we should fall and have a mud bath.

My last day in Bario was a visual feast as I witnessed the celebration of Malaysia's 26th National Day on this highland. Held at the secondary school football field, the morning parade was a rich display of traditional Kelabit costumes: women in their colorful sarong kebaya and bead caps, and men in their batik shirts and straw hats adorned with hornbill feathers. Apart from them, the primary school children turned up in their usual school uniforms; the older ones were holding their bamboo musical instruments, waiting for their turn to perform the piece of music that Raja and I heard by chance the day before. There was joy written on everybody's face, from the youngest pupil to the oldest man in the village; they were all celebrating the nation's birthday. Their cheerful countenance more than made up for the lack of precision and uniformity in their marching. As the primary school pupils filed past the grandstand, I noticed that some of them did not wear shoes. Nonetheless, they were earnest in their participation as a contingent. There was no sense of shame on their faces but pure innocence and joy. That spirit characterized Bario.

I departed from Bario after the celebration. Through three connecting flights, I returned to my clean and orderly country on the same day. What went through my mind as I journeyed back to Singapore were images of simplicity and joy, natural beauty and harmony; what remained firmly etched in my heart was the hospitality of the people, from the army personnel stationed in Bario to the inhabitants of the various longhouses that I visited. I also thanked God for bringing the rain to delay my departure from Bario by one day so that I could be a privileged spectator of the National Day celebration.

My time in the Kelabit highlands was truly priceless and serendipitous. I had originally planned to scale Mount Kinabalu but my focus was somehow diverted to trek in the remote Kelabit highlands. The experience had caused me once again to appreciate simple things in life and to delight in the God who created this gem - Kelabit highlands. Above all, I was glad to learn from the Kelabit Christians the discipline of waking early for morning prayers, a discipline that is largely elusive in modern cities and advanced countries.

Map 6 : England & Scotland

CHAPTER 11

Discovering the Beauty of England and Scotland

By day the Lord directs his love, at night his song is with me — a prayer to the God of my life.

Psalm 42:8

Within a week after my departure from Bario, I was back in the United Kingdom for one last year. As part of the scholarship contract, I was to receive training to become a certified teacher through the Postgraduate Certificate in Education (PGCE) programme run by the Education department of Loughborough University. Knowing that this would be my final year as a student in the United Kingdom, I was intent on discovering the beauty of this country which had over the past years become my second home.

In retrospect, this year of training to be a certified teacher was the most intense and challenging of all my years as a student. Not only did I have to attend classes and complete assignments like all other university students, I also had to observe experienced teachers conduct classes at the local schools assigned to me, and then teach some classes on my own. All in all, I had three weeks of attachment at an elementary school in Loughborough, another three weeks at Ipstock Community College, and finally eleven weeks of teaching practice at Garendon High School in Loughborough. In particular, the eleven-week teaching practice kept me on my toes as my two teaching supervisors—one for Physical Education and one for English -- could visit me at the school anytime to observe my teaching, without giving me any prior notice. In addition, I was also fighting against the prejudice that a Chinese without the British accent could not possibly teach English in a high school in England. The odds were stacked against me, and I seriously needed help.

I was ever conscious of my predicament during this teaching practice year, and it caused me to lean even closer to God. On the first Sunday after returning to Loughborough, 10th Sep 1989, I went to church and sang a hymn which defined my relationship with God for the rest of my time in England—'What a friend we have in Jesus'. The hymn comforted me; the lyrics spoke to me. I copied the entire hymn in my diary to remind myself to carry everything to God in prayer. The first stanza of the hymn reads as follows:

> What a friend we have in Jesus,
> All our sins and griefs to bear;
> What a privilege to carry
> Ev'rything to God in prayer.
> Oh, what peace we often forfeit,
> Oh, what needless pain we bear –

All because we do not carry
Ev'rything to God in prayer.

I was also keenly aware of my need for spiritual fellowship with which to grow in intimacy with God. In the month of November 1989, I participated in two Christian retreats over two weekends in the Peak District; the first was with the Loughborough Chinese Christian Fellowship at Hartington Youth Hostel and the second with the William Morris Hall Christian Fellowship at Meerbrook Youth Hostel. Together, such retreats had the effect of drawing me closer to the word of God and the fellowship of believers.

The month-long Christmas vacation saw me reading and meditating on God's word and Christian literature. One of the books I devoured was *My Searching Heart* by the author Crying Wind. In this autobiographical account, the author shared her personal experience of encountering God, and one of the narrative episodes spoke to me directly:

"'Fix it, Mommy!' he sobbed.
He handed me the truck but kept the wheels.
'Son, you have to give me all the pieces, or I can't fix it.'
Suddenly, I knew that I had been asking God to 'fix' my problem, but I hadn't turned over all the pieces. Now I knew I had to turn the whole thing over to God.

"My son handed the wheels to me, and in a second, I snapped them into place. The toy was as good as new, and he went back to his play."

Like the author's son, I had to surrender all my cares—academic, social, and spiritual--to God. I must not hold back anything from Him.

In such a meditative mood, I celebrated my 24th birthday in January 1990. In self-imposed solitary confinement, I penned a poem to mark God's grace to me in the past year. It had been a full year since my return from New York and my internal emotional struggle to release K from my heart. As I reflected on the year, my heart welled up with gratitude for the spiritual growth that God had blessed me with.

Lines Composed on My 24th Birthday

The glory of the sun is shining through
The tree, the symbol of great years and strength;
I gaze and gaze—the birds that sing and sway,
The grass caressed so gently by the wind
That carries little melodies from up
Among the branches. Bare.
                              It's January.
The summation of years gone by, of birth,
And second birth. Twenty-four years of breath,
Breathing out joy and sadness, laughter, tears;
A life not without fervent pray'rs and sins
One winter ago.
                              Now, as I recall,
I see my Father's hand, guiding and shaping
The intervening year. His grace and mercy,
From one degree bein' lifted onto another,
Sing I, of His redeeming love sent forth
From thence, the years to come.

> The clouds roll on,
> The wind now gathers speed, yet stands the tree,
> Still basking in the glory of the sun.
> I know its season shall come round with leaves,
> Showing its growth within. This certain hope
> Have I in Him: He maketh years of growth.

By February that year, I had read a number of biographies and autobiographies written by mature Christians. One was the biography of Hudson Taylor, the founder of China Inland Mission. In a letter to the Wilsons, missionaries to Thailand supported by the church I was attending in Loughborough, I shared with them the wisdom of Hudson Taylor to trust God to provide: 'No fear that His resources will prove unequal to the emergency! And His resources are mine, for He is mine, and is with me and dwells in me.' Undoubtedly, even as I sought to encourage the Wilsons, I was spiritually much lifted by this bold declaration of faith and trust in a God that will meet us at our points of need. With such faith and trust, I was to begin my eleven-week teaching practice at Garendon High School.

I invested a lot of prayer in my teaching practice at Garendon High School. Every morning before going to school, I would quieten myself with God's word and ask Him for strength and wisdom to cope with the day's activities. For a start, it was not easy for me to pronounce all the English names, some of which I had not seen before. I remembered pronouncing 'Aaron' wrongly, to the amusement of the class. In English classes, I had to get used to different accents; in Physical Education classes, I had to be mindful of my standing position so as to keep an eye on all the students running about in the multi-purpose hall, and to ensure that students were on task and not idling around. It was a steep learning curve for me, especially in the first few weeks; the challenges caused me to lean closer to God.

After six weeks of teaching practice, I was glad to have two weeks of Easter break. Tim, a fellow student at Loughborough University, was going to drive home in his blue Mini to Scotland, and Selvam and I asked to ride along to explore Scotland. We drove to Edinburgh where we attended a Sunday service at Elim Pentecostal Church and then visited the surrounding undulating countryside where we saw more sheep than people. The nature that I had appreciated in Peak District in England was tame and gentrified in comparison to the vastness and ruggedness of the landscape in Scotland.

After two nights in Edinburgh, Selvam and I bade farewell to Tim and continued our journey in Scotland. Armed with a British map, some drawing papers and whiteboard markers with which to indicate our intended direction of travel, we decided to hitch rides going northward via the A9 motorway. Positioning ourselves at appropriate junctions, we were able to get three rides: the first brought us to Perth; the second, Dunkeld; and the last, Inverness. We covered a road distance of about 250 km that day. The verse that I read that day was taken from Psalm 42:8 which says, 'By day the Lord directs his love, at night his song is with me – a prayer to the God of my life.' Indeed, God provided kind souls to pick us up at different junctures in the day, and our response at the end of the day was a song of praise welling up from the bottom of our hearts.

Upon the recommendation of the locals, we decided to spend the next day visiting the Loch Ness Centre &

Exhibition located some 25 km southwest of Inverness. Hitching part of the way and walking the rest of the distance along Lake Ness, we found ourselves poring over the exhibits which focused on the geological formation of the lake and its legendary lochness monster. Although the existence of the monster was not conclusively proven, the folklore surrounding it nevertheless gave the lake an aura of mystery which enchanted many locals and visitors alike. After the educational visit, we hitched back to Inverness where we roamed around the town centre before warming ourselves at the fireplace of the Bed and Breakfast where we were spending the night.

The next day, emboldened by our success in the past two days, we were determined to hitch further north to the northern coast of Scotland. This time, God provided an Italian couple to pick us up just before the Kessock Bridge outside of Inverness. We drove up the A9 motorway along the scenic east coast, passing by picturesque villages like Tain, Golspie, and Brora to arrive at Helmsdale, where we took a left turn up A897 to Kinbrace, then B871 to Syre before reaching the village of Tongue on the north-western coast of Scotland. It was a long and relaxing drive through the rugged mountains and grasslands, made more interesting by the sight of highland cattle, a Scottish breed of rustic cattle with long horns and a long shaggy brown coat. The long furry coat no doubt keeps the animal warm in such harsh highland conditions.

The village of Tongue was a perfect picture of stillness. After checking into the only youth hostel here, a stone lodge situated on the shores of the Kyle of Tongue, Selvam and I went for a walk in this village to soak in the peculiar atmosphere of remoteness and tranquility. Nothing seemed to be moving or have moved; everything appeared to be fixed in time and space, like the objects in an oil painting or an old photograph. There was a noticeable absence of human beings and locomotives, of the hustle and bustle of life in towns and cities; instead, sheep dotted the vast and open landscape, reminding us that we had arrived at the farthest edge of Scotland where time seemingly stood still.

Much as we enjoyed the stillness of life in Tongue, we were ready to hit the road again the next morning. This time, we were heading south. The first ride brought us to Lairg where we had a cup of hot chocolate to warm our bodies and subsequently to Bonar Bridge; the second ride transported us to Inverness where we had earlier spent two nights; and the third to a youth hostel along Loch Ness. As hitchhikers, we did not have the liberty to ask the drivers to stop every now and then for us to capture the beauty of the scenery. Fortunately for us, those who gave us rides did stop occasionally to photograph the breathtaking landscape; in this way, I had the opportunity to take photos of the azure blue waters of Loch Shin. That evening, my reading of the Bible brought me to Psalm 92, and I recorded verse 2 in my diary: 'to proclaim your love in the morning and your faithfulness at night.' Certainly, God was faithful in providing rides to take us to the farthest northwestern village of Tongue, and then all the way back to Loch Ness.

The next day was Good Friday. It turned out to be a day of testing of our faith, a day filled with desperation and earnest prayer. It drizzled almost continuously from the early morning. We waited two hours along the road just outside the youth hostel for a car to pick us up. Though we were sufficiently clothed, the wind chilled our faces and fingers. Just when we were giving up hope of hitching a ride on a wet and chilly morning, a car pulled up next to us. The driver, a Scottish mountain rescuer, was on his way to Fort William to scale Ben Nevis, the highest peak in Britain. He brought us to Fort William, where another driver brought us 8 miles further south to Corran Ferry Point. From here, a rather easy-going young man offered us a ride and transported us south through Glasgow onto the M74 motorway, stopping just outside the town of Hamilton. By then, it was half past six in the evening, and the remaining daylight hours were limited. After some indecision and deliberation, we decided to look for a Bed and Breakfast nearby.

Following some signage, we walked a couple of kilometres into Hamilton, unsure where exactly we were heading towards. Both of us were tired, hungry and desperate for a place to rest our weary bodies. However, within us, we believed that we were left in Hamilton for a purpose. At Hamilton Central railway station, Selvam had the intention to return to Loughborough and thus checked the price of a single train ticket from Hamilton to Loughborough. He was disgusted to find it cost more than forty pounds. Then we went to enquire the timetable and fare from the coach station directly opposite the railway station. The fare was more reasonable; moreover, the coach was leaving late at night for the Midlands, which meant saving on accommodation for that night. Glad to have this option to end our trip, though I was more inclined to continue hitchhiking, we went to withdraw some money from a bank auto-teller machine to buy a big 'Four Seasons' pizza which we devoured in the waiting room of the railway station.

Shortly after we had finished eating, four local youths stumbled into the waiting room. One of them was visibly sick, possibly unwell as a result of excessive drinking, and was vomiting. Urgh! The other three were busy preparing sticks of cigarette from some kind of tobacco, which I overheard cost 15 pounds for a small packet. They were not in any way destructive or abusive; they were just youths without a sense of purpose in life, misguided in their beliefs that they were living life to the fullest. A short while later, a bigger group of youths came into the room with bottles of beer or whisky in their hands. Unlike the earlier group, this group had absolutely no sense of proper behaviour and conduct in public. They traded abusive language with one another and even harassed some ladies. As though to create a climax, one of them threw an empty beer bottle into the glass panel of a shelter, cheering as it broke into smithereens.

Misguided youths steeped in alcoholism. We witnessed firsthand the destructive effects of alcohol on the youths and we momentarily understood why God had placed us in Hamilton: God wanted us to pray for these youths and intercede for their salvation. God so loved the youths of Scotland that He brought us there to witness their disorientation so that we might pray with knowledge and fervency for them. For this purpose, the few hours we spent in Hamilton Central railway station were worth it.

At 11.25 p.m. Selvam bought for himself a coach ticket heading for Birmingham (which is near to Loughborough) since I wished to continue hitchhiking. As I saw him board the bus near midnight, a sense of panic came over me; internally, I was asking myself, 'What do I do? Where do I spend the night?' At that moment, a couple who had just seen their son board another coach bound for London walked past me. Instinctively, I called out to them, explained my situation, that I was a student hitchhiking on a shoestring budget, and asked if I could put up at their house for a night. Without much thought, the man said, 'C'mon!' As he drove back to his house in Wishaw, some 10 km from Hamilton, I was praising God at the back of the car. God showed me His love and provision in Hamilton: I asked and He provided, immediately.

How wonderful was the Lord's provision: supper, hot shower, a warm bed, and breakfast the following day. At 10 a.m., my benefactor, Mr Welsh, drove me to Motherwell, an adjacent town next to the M74 motorway, to wait for a lift heading south into England. Before I got off the car, he placed both his hands on my right arm and reassured me that everything would turn out alright. I thanked him profusely for his hospitality; inwardly, I kept singing praises to God for using him to bless me.

But this state of exultation did not last long. As the cold wind came along with the drizzle, and the hour wore on, I began to shiver and moan in my heart. A battle arose within me: a part of me wanted to stand there and continue to wait for a ride; the other part yearned to look for a better spot with a higher probability of being picked up. I stood there and vacillated between the two options. Much later, a man came to point me in the direction that I should go, to a service station. I took his word as God's direction for me and walked for half a mile in the cold wind and needle-sharp rain, but no service station was within sight. Not wishing to wander on aimlessly, I turned back; half of my hope died.

The ensuing hour was marked by an internal struggle to gain self-control and then to surrender to God. Despite my trying to hitch a ride from different road junctions, nobody stopped to pick me up. Suddenly, a frightful thought came to mind: God wanted me to stay there for another day!

> 'For what?' I struggled and argued within me.
> 'He would reveal later,' a voice within me said.
> 'But where am I going to spend the night?'
> 'Has He not been faithful the night before and rescued you?'

I knew He had. Still, I did not want to stay. I fought against the thought; I cried. Then I remembered that He uses those who are available and blesses those who are obedient. Finally, I surrendered. I allowed Him to dictate and run my life; I submitted myself to Him, without reservation. Soon after yielding my will to God, three successive kind souls offered me a lift: first, a youth worker brought me to Carlisle, an English city near the border with Scotland; then, a lawyer drove me to Penrith, a town just outside the famous Lake District; and lastly, a prison officer brought me to Keswick, a scenic town in the Lake District. Once again, God proved His faithfulness in providing rides for me.

In Keswick, I was to experience another special provision by God. Arriving at such a popular touristy town on the day before Easter Sunday without any hostel reservation was a recipe for disaster. I enquired at several hostels and they were all fully booked for the weekend. However, I still cherished hope in my heart as I reminded myself of God's faithfulness. After being turned away by many hostels, I decided to return to the first youth hostel I approached so that I might make telephone enquiries for a vacant bed in other hostels from there. To my delight, as I stepped into the youth hostel, I was informed by the receptionist that there was a last-minute cancellation of a bed in the male dormitory. God made all things possible! Hallelujah!

Not only did God provide a bed for me in Kewsick, He also gave me company in the form of two girls: Jackie from England and Edu from Spain. I met them while ambling around the town, and we had tea together before attending a talk on the mountains and fells of Lake District. We also met up the next day, Easter Sunday, for a hike from Keswick to Thirlmere Youth Hostel. It was a gradual climb from Keswick to High Seat, a mountain peak situated in between Derwentwater Lake and Thirlmere Lake. From the vantage point, we went downhill in an easterly direction till we reached the western shore of Thirlmere Lake. Thereafter, it was a rather easy walk around the northern edge of the lake to the youth hostel. The entire hike took about six hours during which we weathered through occasional sunshine, rain and wind. Though the weather was less than ideal, we enjoyed the hike, the nature around us and one another's company. It was my first introduction to the Lake District, and a very memorable one.

The next morning, God granted me the desire of my heart to visit the Dove Cottage in Grasmere. In this cottage, the famous English poet William Wordsworth and his sister Dorothy once lived, from December 1799 to May 1808. It was while living here that he produced most of his best-loved poems. I remembered reading the poem *The World is Too Much with Us* in my secondary school Literature class, and many more in my second year of university when I studied Romantic poets. Among my favourite Wordsworth's poems were *Michael*, a pastoral poem about the plight of an old shepherd, *I Wandered*

Lonely as a Cloud, a lyric poem in praise of nature, and *The Prelude*, an autobiographical poem that chronicles the life of the poet from his childhood days to his identification with the French Revolution. Visiting the Dove Cottage was to me a dream come true. With nobody to hurry me along, I spent hours poring over the manuscripts and memorabilia in this cottage-turned-museum. The visit marked the end of my Easter trip and once again, I relied on God to hitchhike back to Loughborough.

God never fails to provide, though sometimes we have to wait. After waiting for about an hour, three Australian girls picked me up and gave me a ride from Grasmere to a service station in Stoke on Trent. They were on a working vacation in England and had taken time off to visit the Lake District over the Easter weekend. Then a gentleman with a cigar, who introduced himself as a divorcee living with a mistress, brought me from the service station to Ashby de la Zouch. The final leg of the journey was provided through a family living in Loughborough. They drove me straight to William Morris Hall. Praise the Lord! Indeed, as the psalmist says in Psalm 13:6, 'I will sing to the Lord, for he has been good to me.'

The past ten days in Scotland and the Lake District had not only been therapeutic but also faith-building. The change in scenery each day had the effect of taking my mind off the rigorous demands of my teaching practice; it had also drawn me closer to nature and to God. My faith in God as the provider of all my needs was severely tested and strengthened on this trip. I struggled to let God take control of my life, and when I eventually did let go and let God reign supreme in my life, He made all things beautiful. He supplied lifts to bring me to the Lake District, kept a bed for me in Keswick over the busy Easter weekend, and even provided me with company to go on a hike. In addition, He also gave me the opportunity to fulfill the desire of my heart to visit the Dove Cottage and brought me back to the doorstep of my hall of residence in Loughborough.

With renewed strength and faith in God, I resumed my teaching practice in Garendon High School. In my heart, I had such blessed assurance of His abiding love and presence in all that I had to accomplish in the remaining five weeks in Garendon. Above the normal teaching timetable, I assisted in the school's lunch time sporting activities and a poetry evening. As the weeks went by, my relationships with the cooperating teachers and students improved so much so that on the last day of my stint there, the school awarded me a commendation certificate. I was glad that the challenging period of teaching practice was finally over, but more importantly, I rejoiced that through the tough times, my faith in God had increased manifold.

I made use of the remaining weeks in England to see more of the countryside, and to spend time with the spiritual community in Loughborough that I had grown to love. My former secondary school mate and fellow scout, also a Christian, Gerald, who was studying in the United States then, came to visit me right after the end of my teaching practice. Together, we had fellowship and cycled from Loughborough through Hinckley, Coventry and Leamington to Stratford-upon-Avon, the birthplace of William Shakespeare, where we watched a play entitled *The Last Days of Don Juan*. The 100 km that we covered each way on our bicycles allowed us time to appreciate the immense beauty of the English countryside. Two weeks later, I also joined the Loughborough Chinese Christian Fellowship on a trip to explore North York Moors where

I saw more of the rustic English landscape punctuated with magnificent castles and abbeys. More than the fair sight of nature and architecture, I valued the fellowship of other Christians.

My last days in England were also marked with special occasions. One was the 60th birthday celebration of Joan Robertson. She had been a motherly figure to me all these years in Loughborough and I was privileged to be one of the guests at the celebration. The other key event was the marriage of my Singaporean friend Anthony to a British girl, Lyn. It took place in Lavenham, Suffolk, on a warm day in mid-July. The joyous and spirit-filled occasion was witnessed by many from Loughborough, including the Booklesses, Joan, and many from the Loughborough Chinese Christian Fellowship. The following day, back in Elim Church in Loughborough, Selvam and I were prayed for by the elders of the church as they released us to complete our national service back in Singapore.

I left Loughborough with many fond memories of the lovely people who had in one way or another contributed to my faith in God. In the past four years, I had gained not only a bachelor's degree, a teaching certification, and international exposure to people from diverse countries and backgrounds, but also wisdom in knowing and trusting God. With such wisdom, I was ready to tackle my next phase of life in the army back in Singapore.

Map 7 : India & Pakistan

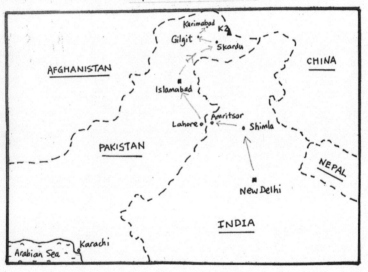

CHAPTER 12

Exploring India and Pakistan

May he give you the desire of your heart and make all your plans succeed.

Psalm 20:4

I had the desire to spend some time with the British missionary family in Thailand that I had occasionally corresponded with before returning to Singapore for good. Thus, I booked a London-to-Singapore air ticket with Thai Airways which allowed me to stop over in Thailand for two weeks. However, just before I departed from England, I received news that the family was not able to receive me during that period of time. Not wishing to change my booking and incur more cost, I decided to explore Thailand on my own.

I spent a greater part of the two weeks in northern Thailand. First, I joined a local tour which brought us trekking in the different tribal villages: Karen, Akha, and Lahu. In some villages, I came face to face with people smoking opium and worshipping spirits; I prayed for them in my heart. Then I ventured further north to Mae Sai and even crossed the border illegally into Myanmar with the help of some Burmese working in Mae Sai. I experienced firsthand the corruption of policemen near the Golden Triangle but also the hospitality of some Burmese in Tachileik, the border town in Myanmar. On the second Sunday, I had the opportunity to attend two church services in Bangkok and listened to God's word.

I returned to Singapore on 1st August, 1990. One of my main priorities was to settle down and grow in a local church; the other was to acclimatize to the hot and humid weather. Together with Selvam, I joined one of the fastest growing churches in Singapore then and participated in cell group meetings during the mid-week. To prepare myself physically to return to military life for another year, I chose to run during noon time. Within a month, I was re-enlisted and posted back to my former army unit, 3rd Battalion Guards, as a company 2nd in command. Overall, I adjusted well and enjoyed the interaction with other officers and soldiers; at times, informally, I even discussed the existence of God with some of the officers. As the military training program so dictated, I found myself going to Brunei for jungle training for the third time.[29] Tough as the training was, I made good use of the lull time in between field exercises to read and study God's word.

---

[29] The first time I went to Brunei was as an officer cadet; the second time was as a platoon commander in 3rd Battalion Guards before I disrupted my National Service for university.

Before the end of my one-year national service in early August 1991, I had made plans to visit some missionaries in India on my way to join an Operation Raleigh expedition in Chile which would begin in late September. The church that I had joined in Singapore was and still is a mission-minded church with many believers being sent out to other countries to plant churches. Having missed the opportunity to work with the British missionaries in Thailand a year ago, I was excited about visiting and learning more from those serving in India, and of course I would also like to travel a little in the Indian sub-continent. With this in mind, I booked a Singapore-to-London[30] return air ticket with Aeroflot, a Russian airline, which would allow me to stop over in India for five weeks.

My ignorance and lack of research on the public holidays in India caused me to land in New Delhi on 15 August, India's Independence Day. It was the worst day to arrive at the capital of India as the entire nation would congregate in the city to celebrate the nation's Independence Day. That meant that all the hotels would be fully booked. By the time I cleared the immigration and emerged from the airport, it was close to mid-night, a most inconvenient time. I managed to catch the last public bus leaving the airport for the city and had absolutely no idea where it was heading. The streets were dimly lit; here and there, as the bus negotiated some corners, I saw dark angular human figures sitting or lying on roadsides and below flyovers—they were probably the homeless people of this mega city. After alighting from the bus at the bus

---

[30] Team members of the expedition to Chile had to gather in London before flying together to Chile.

terminal, I walked into a dingy hotel only to be told that all the rooms were occupied. I was, however, shown a small windowless room with a ceiling fan, probably a makeshift storeroom, which was still available. Given the lateness of the hour, I readily accepted it though the heat in the room was unbearable.

This rude introduction to India did not dampen my spirits the next day. When daylight broke, I ventured out onto the streets with my camera to familiarize myself with this new city. The narrow streets were devoid of trees; concrete slabs and stones lined the sides, and one must be watchful not to kick a stone or fall into one of the uncovered holes along the way. Despite this haphazard development, the place was alive with human activities. I saw a boy filling a jelly can with water from a roadside tap, a young lady having her hand painted with henna[31], queues forming at a public milk dispenser, parents jostling for space outside a narrow school gate to pass food and drinks to their children, and people walking in the middle of a road while yellow-topped auto rickshaws negotiated to the right and left of them, oblivious to the commercial banners hanging overhead proclaiming sales of various products. After weaving in and out of various alleyways to take interesting photos, I returned to the hotel to collect my baggage and hailed an auto rickshaw to take me to the missionaries.

The rickshaw driver brought me to Mukherjee Nagar in the northern part of the city. Here, I managed to locate the apartment wherein the missionaries lived. Renting the

---

[31] A reddish-brown dye made from the powdered leaves of a tropical shrub, used to decorate the body, especially the hands of ladies.

entire level three of the house, the four single missionaries, two male and two female, operated as a team to reach out to the residents nearby with the gospel. Their targets included shopkeepers, rickshaw drivers, the young and the old, the working class, as well as the more educated professionals. To converse effectively with locals, they hired a Hindi teacher to give them language classes on a regular basis. On Sundays, the living room was converted into a church sanctuary where the preaching of God's word took place.

As a temporary member of the team, I had the privilege to follow some of them as they made their regular house visits to those who welcomed them. In a typical house, one could easily find pictures of Hindu gods displayed on the walls of the house. To encourage these people to know Bible scriptures, one of the strategies was to give them beautiful Christian posters with God's promises so that they could display the posters on the walls. Above all, it was the team's genuine care and concern for the people that touched their hearts. On one such visit, we called on an Afghan family seeking refugee status in India. They received the team warmly and narrated to us their harrowing escape from the Taliban.

From my observation, being a missionary in a foreign land is no easy task. Not only does it call for a surrender of the comfort of home and even one's career, it also involves cross-cultural living – learning and speaking a new language and adopting the practices of a new culture. Above all, a missionary must identify with the local people and live like one of them, befriend them, and share the love of God with them, even if they be poor, homeless, stateless, and despised by the majority. It is not an endeavor for the faint-hearted and those who lack commitment and a sense of calling.

After spending almost a week with the four missionaries, I was itching to travel beyond the confines of New Delhi. So I booked a berth on a night train travelling from Delhi to Kalka. It was my first train journey in India and the most unforgettable one. Along the route, the train called at many stations, picking up more passengers while allowing some to disembark. The monotony of the routine soon put me to sleep in my berth. However, in the middle of the night, I felt somebody pushing against my body. As I opened my eyes, I was horrified to find a body sharing my berth. In a state of shock and fury, I ordered the man to get down immediately. He did. In my mind, this man had violated my rights and privacy in the berth for which I had paid to spend the night, and he had absolutely no rights to share the space with me without my consent. Long after the incident, I often asked myself if I would behave the same way as that opportunistic man if I had grown up a poor peasant constantly needing to fight for survival in the world's second most populous country. I probably would.

The shock of having my privacy invaded in the middle of the night soon gave way to a sense of calm and normalcy as the train pulled into Kalka in the early hours of the following day. I saw many licensed porters in red standing and squatting near the platform, waiting to be hired. Nearby, a man operating a tea stall on wheels was waiting for customers to patronize him. For these porters and peddlers, the arrival of trains meant more business and income for them with which they support themselves and their families. For some, this might be their way of life from one generation to another as licenses were often passed down the generations, from fathers to sons or sons–in–law[32].

After a brief stopover at Kalka, I hopped onto another train bound for Shimla, the capital of the northern Indian state of Himachal Pradesh and the former summer capital of British India. The train journey is one of the most scenic in the country. The train negotiated slowly along the curvy edges of the southern Himalayan foothills, gaining 1620 metres in height from start to finish. Enroute, it made several stops for passengers to embark and disembark, and some stops were even long enough for passengers to have a cup of hot tea amidst the fresh mountain air.

Shimla has a blend of British and Indian flavor. Walking along Mall Road, the main shopping belt, one could see signage in both English and Hindi, and retail shops, cafes and banks housed in two–storey British architecture, characterized by the use of red bricks and timber. Along The Ridge, a paved promenade where no cars were allowed, one could see statues of revered Indian politicians such as Mahamat Gandhi, India's spiritual leader during the country's struggle against Britain for home rule, and Indira Gandhi, India's first and to date, the only female prime minister. However, apart from the vestige of English architecture in Shimla, the people moving about in the city were clearly Indian by race and costume, and the products sold in the shops were distinctly Indian. It seemed that besides the physical structures, the Indian government had eradicated British influence from Shimla.

---

[32] Extracted from https://www.thehindu.com/features/metroplus/men–in–red/article4999375.ece

The Indian culture in Shimla was pervasive. I spent two more days in the vicinity of Shimla, in Summer Hill and Jakhu Hill, and witnessed the vibrancy of life of the people. From porters to merchants to little children to university students, almost everybody I came across looked Indian and dressed like an Indian. I did not meet many foreign tourists, nor did I see children of mixed parentage, like the Eurasians[33] in Singapore. In this largely Hindu country, where traditional caste system is still valued by the majority, inter-caste marriages were hardly heard of, not to mention inter-racial marriages.[34] However, I did meet some Tibetan-looking peddlers of textiles on Jakhu Hill who were friendly enough to talk to me and pose for photographs. Overall, Shimla was homogeneous in terms of its ethnic composition.

The homogeneity of the people was more pronounced as I travelled westward to the city of Amritsar in the neigbouring state of Punjab. Here, almost every Punjabi man wore a turban on his head and kept long unshorn hair, while every Punjabi woman had a veil over her head. There was a strong sense of religiosity in the way they dressed and conducted themselves. This strict adherence to Sikhism was most evident in the Golden Temple, the most significant Sikh temple in the world, where I visited since it was listed as a must-see place in Amritsar. Outside the temple, I saw a big billboard on which were words exhorting the population to practice the virtues of different religions, that "they shape persons inclined

---

[33] They have mixed parentage, usually the father is from a European country and the mother is from South-east Asia.

[34] Extracted   from   https://paa2011.princeton.edu/papers/111966

to excessive indulgence into cultured men and women."
And just below that was another quotation by Sri Jayendra
Sarswati, a famous guru: "Every Sikh should be taught
about his daily religious duties. Only such religiously
cultivated mind would make a person disciplined."

The visit to the Golden Temple was quite an
intimidating one. At one of the four main entrances to
the temple, three stern-looking Punjabi men dressed in
light blue uniform were on guard duty, keeping an eye
on the people entering the temple, and one of them had a
long spear in his hands. Beyond the entrance, I saw men
and women sitting along a corridor, presumably waiting
for their turns to enter the holy pool or waiting for their
loved ones to finish performing some rituals. As I walked
further in, I saw some men, fully dressed, standing almost
motionless in the pool with the water reaching up to their
thighs, while at another end of the pool, a group of elderly
men, stripped down to their waists, were preparing to
enter the pool. There was no commotion or excitement
in their rituals, just a sense of awe and reverence as they
prayed in the pool. The water from the pool is believed to
be holy and to have healing powers; thus, some devotees
would bottle the water and bring it home for their sick
friends and relatives.

Much as I found the visit to Amritsar an eye-opener,
I was glad to leave the city, and the general sense of
'unfriendliness' it inspired, in a train bound for Lahore
in Pakistan. As the train crossed the border from India
into Pakistan, a sense of relief came over me as the
claustrophobia of India gave way to open fields where
donkeys grazed. At the Lahore railway station, a gentle
and friendly man greeted me as I emerged from the
station. He showed me a name card with 'Youth Guest

House' printed on it and quoted me 50 Pakistani rupees (slightly more than US$2) for a night. As he claimed that the guest house was only about 6 minutes' walk from the station, I willingly followed him. Though the room was rather bare, it was clean and came with an overhead fan. I readily accepted it. My first priority then was to have a shower—what a relief it was after experiencing all that heat and dust, and countless flies at Atari, the border town in India. After freshening up, I went out to buy a copy of the local newspaper in English to familiarize myself with the political, economic and social issues of this country.

My main interest was to travel in the remote north-eastern part of Pakistan. Therefore, without spending more time to explore Lahore, I took a train the next morning and headed north to Rawalpindi, the neighboring and twin city of Islamabad, the capital city of Pakistan. Here, I met a fellow solo traveler, Lun, from Hong Kong. As both of us had the interest to see the remote north, we decided to take a flight together to Skardu, the starting point of any mountaineering expedition to conquer K2, the second highest peak in the world. I thanked God for this fortuitous meeting with Lun, who provided me not only with company but also a means to save accommodation cost.

On the day of our flight from Rawalpindi to Skardu, we had to wake at half past three in the morning to pack our bags. Through the help of a local driver, we managed to hire a taxi to fetch us to the airport for 25 Pakistani rupees (slightly more than US$1). The early morning flight to Skardu was spectacular. The pilot flew the plane just above the clouds, and occasionally we could see the Himalayan mountain peaks just below us. At some points, it seemed that the wings of the aircraft were rubbing against some crags. Finally, after hovering above the clouds for about an hour, the plane landed in Skardu, in the bosom of the Skardu valley with huge mountains towering all around it.

Skardu, a city in the province of Gilgit-Baltistan in Pakistan, is situated 2438 metres above sea level. Despite the sudden increase of about 2000 metres in altitude from Rawalpindi to Skardu, we did not experience any altitude sickness. After checking into a hotel, we explored the streets of Skardu with our cameras. Even though the surrounding landscape was dry and barren, there were large quantities of fresh vegetables on sale in the market: onion, cucumber, tomato, cabbage and turnip. These supplies must have come from more fertile neighboring provinces. As we walked around the residential areas, we saw children who were sufficiently dressed, well fed and cheerful, a sign that poverty was far from this city. We also climbed up the Kharpocho Fort fronting the Indus River, from which we had a magnificent view of the valley.

It was my habit to write to my family and friends as I travelled. At a new place, I would usually buy some local postcards and send them to those I wished to share my joy with. One of the many I wrote to at Skardu was Janet, the younger daughter of the Crowhurst family:

> "This is the capital of Baltistan, perched 7,500 feet above sea-level, in the bosom of the great peaks of the Karakoram mountain range. Mountaineers who intend to scale K2, the second highest peak in the world, have to begin their land journey from Skardu. It is a most charming town. The people are friendly

and the awesome beauty of the towering peaks and the cool running streams is beyond ordinary description. This morning, I went for a haircut, which cost about 25 pence, and walked down to the stream just below my hotel room for a wash and a dip. It was life at its most simple, natural and carefree form. I suddenly recalled a Haiku (a short Japanese poem) I wrote some years back in Loughborough:

> The mountain ranges,
> Rising, ebbing, beckoning
> My inner being.

With that, my belated birthday wishes to you. Matt 21:21."

One distinct difference between India and Pakistan that I noticed was the presence or absence of women in public areas. Whilst women were commonly seen in Shimla and Amritsar, they were almost 'invisible' in Skardu. Along the streets of Skardu, only men in their traditional Pakistani costumes could be seen walking along the streets; in the nearby streams, only boys could be seen frolicking in the water. All the women and girls seemed to have been hidden at home! One late afternoon, Lun and I came across a group of children playing in an open sandy area. They were mostly boys, about a dozen of them, aged between six and twelve. On seeing us, some of them began saying 'Bruce Lee' and posed in a kung fu stance. I was surprised that even in this remote place, the name of Bruce Lee was known! While we did not play along with them, we encouraged them to pose for photographs in kung fu stances. They readily obliged and exuded much joy and confidence in their poses.

After two days in Skardu, Lun and I decided to travel in a local mini-bus along the provincial highway of S-1 in a north-westerly direction to Gilgit. The bus moved almost parallel to the Indus River, covering a ground distance of 208 km in more than four hours. At times, the meandering mountain road we were travelling on was 50 or more metres vertically above the gushing Indus River, and a slight mistake by the bus driver could mean the entire bus falling head-on into the river below. The precipitous landscape did not cause fear in me; instead, I was awe-struck by the majesty of the geographical features all around me.

Gilgit is a city situated in a broad valley near the confluence of Gilgit River and Hunza River. With an elevation of 1500 metres above sea level, it is a major tourist destination and entry point for trekking and mountaineering expeditions in the Karakoram mountain range. On arrival at the city centre, I saw four young children seated quietly on a bench in a shop, well-dressed and wide-eyed, each sipping a bottle of Fanta orange soda drink. On the wall behind them was a big poster of the K2 brand cigarette. This scene spoke of the affluence of the city of Gilgit, where imported goods were readily available for consumption. In this city, I also saw roadside peddlers selling spices and grains, and shops offering chicken and eggs; there was no shortage of food in this remote city in northern Pakistan. Again, I noticed that men and men only thronged the streets and patronized the stalls.

Acting on the advice of some locals, Lun and I went trekking up some mountain paths. Soon, we were rewarded with a spectacular view of the snow-capped Rakaposhi mountain in the Karakoram mountain range. Standing at 7788 metres above sea level, the Rakaposhi peak is visible even in Gilgit, which is located approximately 40 km to the south. In Gilgit, we also came across numerous huge wooden suspension bridges on which the local men walked or rode on horses, and buses wobbled slowly across. Momentarily, we seemed to be transported back in time to ancient days when horses were the predominant mode of transport. The bare and brown mountains in the background, together with the costumes and headgear of the men, seemed to suggest a Middle Eastern setting like that of Ali Baba in the Arabian Nights stories. Both of us were excited to explore more of this part of the world. Our exploration brought us further north to Karimabad in the Hunza Valley.

The bus journey from Gilgit to Karimabad taught me an object lesson on valuing human relationships. Before the bus got out of Gilgit, it stopped at various shops along the way for the driver and some passengers to purchase or deliver some goods. It was like a family shopping trip, where different individuals had differing needs and preferences for the things they wanted to buy. I was initially flabbergasted by this 'wastage of time' but was later touched by an incident. At one point along the way, a Hunza woman asked the driver to help her fill her bottle with fresh mountain water from a nearby stream, which the latter obliged. The driver not only did that but also filled his own cup and offered it to some of the bus passengers. A nice touch of personal service! This incident caused me to question the high efficiency that modern city dwellers often pride themselves in having, which often comes at the expense of cultivating human relationships. Perhaps, we need to learn to value and balance both efficiency and relationships, and not sacrifice the latter for the former.

With such thoughts running through my mind, I entered Karimabad and was richly rewarded by its history, culture and character. In terms of history, this town boasts of the iconic Baltit Fort, once the former seat of the Hunza kingdom. Perched on top of a hill at an elevation of about 2500 metres, the structure of the fort resembles somewhat the Potala Palace in Lhasa, suggesting Tibetan influence in its architecture. Lun and I did not visit the fort as it was closed for conservation; instead we spent our time walking and befriending the young inhabitants of this charming hamlet.

Unlike Skardu and Gilgit where women and girls were 'invisible', Karimabad was special. Here, we came across many children, both boys and girls, along the road. They were most friendly to us and agreed to be photographed when asked. In this village, I captured some of the most photogenic shots of children in my entire trip in India and Pakistan. A shy and curious girl with her little sister seated in front of a rock wall; a group of boys seated on a pile of bricks outside a house; a lonesome boy shepherding his flock of four sheep. The best shot was one taken of a boy and a little girl carrying chickens in their arms; their joy and contentment were clearly registered on their smiley faces.

The next day, after a hearty breakfast consisting of eggs, oats and green tea, we took a day trip to Gulmit, some 45 km up the Hunza River. Gulmit is a centuries-old historic town, surrounded by mountains, peaks and glaciers. At the time of our visit, it boasted of a few hotels, shops and a museum which showcased the Hunza culture. From the layout of a typical Hunza hut in the museum, we learned that the people placed great emphasis on music and dancing. The fire place occupied the central part of the hut, dividing the sleeping and dining areas to the left and to the right, and the cooking and dancing areas to the north and to the south. On display were old artifacts such as costumes, weapons, household utensils, musical instruments and a Hunza state flag. It was an educational visit; our only complaint was that the museum was dim and dusty inside, a sign of lack of proper maintenance. For the brief explanations given to us, we were each charged ten Pakistani rupees.

The highlight of our visit to Gulmit, however, was not the visit to the museum but to a girls' school. Totally unexpected, we walked into the school and were greeted by a group of primary school girls in light blue uniform. It was a breath of fresh air to meet these girls with bright eyes and smiley faces. Sensing their friendliness, I introduced myself as a teacher from Singapore to the school authority and was promptly given permission to enter a classroom filled with about 20 slightly older girls. The room was a little dim. There were six long tables and benches in it, three on each side; three to four girls shared a table and a bench. Many of the girls wore white headscarves over their heads. They were attentive to their teacher and were writing something in their exercise books. I asked the male teacher for permission to take photographs of the students and captured their beautiful faces in two shots. It was a rare glimpse into the life of school girls in this country. I was impressed with the authority's vision to educate these young girls, and would have volunteered to teach in this school if not for the fact that I had to move on to join an Operation Raleigh expedition in Chile.

After another night in Karimabad, Lun and I parted ways. He would spend another few days exploring the country before returning to Hong Kong, while I made my way back to New Delhi in India. It was going to be a long journey for me, travelling from Karimabad to Gilgit to Rawalpindi via the Karakoram Highway, and then connecting a train to Lahore, where there would be many options to travel across the international border to New Delhi. The entire journey took up three full days, with two nights spent on board a bus. I did, however, have a Sabbath rest in between on a Sunday, in Lahore, where I connected with my family and friends through postcards and letters, and also attended an evening service at St Andrew's Church.

The voice of God is often heard when one is quiet and meditative. While travelling on a bus along the Karakoram Highway, I heard the little voice of God speaking to me, revealing His beautiful plans for me. I envisaged marriage, in a year or two.[35] I did not understand the vision, for I had nobody special in mind at that point in time, but the vision of marriage came repeatedly to my mind's eye. Not entirely sure if it was from God, I committed the vision to God and placed it at His altar. Then, I was led by the Spirit to read Psalm 20 wherein verse four confirmed God's plans for me, that He will give me the desire of my heart, and make all my plans succeed. And again, the Spirit led me to read Psalm 23 wherein I saw God as my shepherd and provider, with me lacking nothing, not even a life partner. My heart rejoiced at the revelation and I

---

[35] My plan for marriage was confirmed by September 1993, two years from the time of the vision.

proceeded to record it in my diary.[36] As I made the last leg of the long journey, from Lahore to New Delhi, the song 'Abba Father Let Me Be' that was sung in St Andrew's Church in Lahore kept playing in my mind; it became my prayer to God:

> Never let my heart grow cold
> Never let me go
> Abba Father let me be
> Yours and yours alone.

I was glad to rejoin the missionary team in New Delhi after being away for three weeks. Much as I enjoyed wandering in the remote parts of Pakistan, I also had a heart to serve with the missionaries in New Delhi. I participated whole-heartedly in their outreach to the community, calling on different individuals and families throughout the week. At each place of call, we would sing some songs of praise to God in Hindi and read some scriptures from the Bible together with the host family. Each visit was an encouragement for the individual or family to give thanks to God, to commit all concerns to God, and to trust God for the unknown. The team sought to build the faith of others around them, whether they be ethnic Indians, Punjabis, or refugees from Afghanistan; in this way, the team sought to build a church where faithful followers could come together to worship God on Sundays.

In my last ten days in New Delhi, I also had much time to draw close to God through reading the Bible. As

---

[36] Honestly, I completely forgot about this revelation from God till 2021 when I once again read through my diary in order to recall the events of my travel in Pakistan and India.

I looked through the records in my diary, a consistent thread ran through the scriptures that spoke to me: God has chosen me to bear fruit (John 15:16); He wants me to trust Him and remain in whichever place He allows me to dwell in (Psalm 37:3); He also wants me to commit myself to serve Him in neighboring lands (Psalm 76:11). In due obedience, I made a vow and recorded it in my diary, that I would be available for God's use in the neighboring lands of India, such as Pakistan, China, Afghanistan, Nepal, Myanmar and Bhutan.[37]

The last few days in New Delhi were especially busy. In a way, I had to wrap up my experiences in India and Pakistan and prepare myself mentally for the expedition in Chile. As a means to show my gratitude to the team of missionaries who had received me so warmly, I bought the men a shirt each and the ladies a skirt each. I also purchased a Spanish-English phrasebook to teach myself some Spanish words, as Spanish is the national language of Chile. In addition, I also bought some English books; one of them was *Gitanjali*, a collection of poems by the world renowned Bengali poet Rabindranath Tagore, which accompanied me in my voyage in Chile. On the very last evening, the team treated me to a farewell dinner in a Chinese restaurant. It was a warm gesture on their part, showing appreciation for whatever contributions I had made to the team and their ministry.

My brief stint with the missionary team in New Delhi was an eye-opener. Its impact was far- reaching as God used it to prepare me for cross-cultural work in the years ahead.

---

[37] Again, this vow had completely eclipsed my mind till 2021, though subsequent to this vow, I did serve in Nepal for a year and China for six years.

Map 8 : Chile

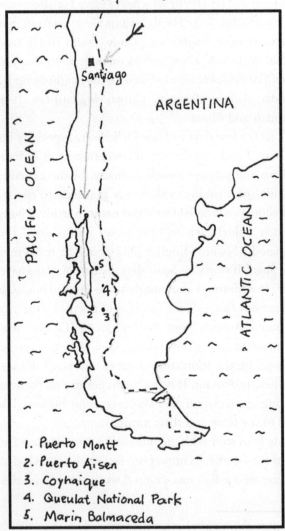

1. Puerto Montt
2. Puerto Aisen
3. Coyhaique
4. Queulat National Park
5. Marin Balmaceda

CHAPTER 13

Of Horses and Snow
in Chile (Part 1)

In his hand are the depths of the earth, and the mountain peaks belong to him.

Psalm 95:4

I left New Delhi on 21st September 1991 with a spirit of excitement. Armed with a Spanish-English phrasebook and a few English books, I was mentally prepared for a long journey to London, enroute stopping at Tashkent and Moscow, and from London to Santiago in Chile via Amsterdam. It would be my first visit to a South American country, and I was eager to learn and use Spanish for the next three months. More than that, I was looking forward to the opportunity to operate on alpine landscape. Though I had survived three times in the dense tropical jungle of Brunei, I had up to then absolutely no experience surviving on snowy grounds as all my travels had thus far been on land up to about 2000 metres above sea level. It would be a brand new experience surviving on snow-capped mountains.

From Santiago, the capital city of Chile, the expedition team took almost three days to travel southward to Coyhaique, the field head-quarter (FHQ) of Operation Raleigh in Chile. First, we travelled by coach from Santiago to Peurto Montt; then we transferred to a ferry sailing in the South Pacific Ocean to Peurto Aisen; finally, we travelled by land again to Coyhaique, which is located at latitude 45.6 degree South, comparable to the southern tip of the South Island of New Zealand on the other side of the South Pacific Ocean. It was truly a long journey in the world's longest country by length from north to south.

As we sailed in the ferry from Peurto Montt to Peurto Aisen, I had copious amount of time to read, reflect and write. I thought about the years spent in Loughborough, the last year in the army, my time in Pakistan and India, and the impending expedition in Chile. It all seemed surreal: from England to Singapore to the Indian sub-continent to southern Chile. I fell into a meditative and languid mood, and composed a poem:

Sailing in Chile

The waves gently folded back,
Glistening in the far horizon, right;
The ferry ploughed on, slowly,
Checking out the length of Chile.

The Patagonian mountains,
Stretching south, thin but wide;
The fair sky, a cloudy white, swayed,
Proclaiming the glory of the day.

I surveyed the land and the sea,
Thinking of words that would delight;
I sat with a pen in my hand,
Writing about this beautiful land.

The entire team comprised about 50 participants and staff who were mostly from the United Kingdom. International participants came from a few countries such as Japan, Singapore and Chile. To facilitate bonding, the team was divided into four smaller groups, each taking on a project at a different location some distance away from the FHQ. All four projects were in operation simultaneously. By the end of the expedition, all groups would have attempted or completed the four different projects.

The first week upon arrival at FHQ was spent on administrative briefing, acclimatization, familiarization with equipment and terrain. We were given lessons on map reading, first aid, pitching of tents, preparing ration, and setting up of a radio set for communication with FHQ. In small groups, we were sent out to practise river crossing, navigation with map and compass, camp craft, rock climbing and trekking in snow. Apart from preparing us for the actual tasks at the different project sites, it was a time for us to bond as we would be working together as a group for the next ten weeks. My group consisted of six male (including me) and four female participants; apart from me, the rest hailed from different parts of the United Kingdom.

My fascination with snow turned into reality in the first week when we went camping in the nearby mountains as part of our acclimatization exercise. One particular night, each of us had to build a bivouac using a groundsheet and whatever tree branch or log we could find. The aim was to build a protective shelter against the wind so that one could sleep comfortably in one's sleeping bag above a sleeping mat in the shelter. Late into the night, when I had settled comfortably in my bivouac, she (the snow) came to visit me. I was thrilled in my spirit and began capturing my feelings on a piece of paper, later fashioned into a poem:

Arrival

The snow flakes and flutters into my bivouac;
I let her rest.
She comes not by invitation, yet
Her coming is not an intrusion.
She lands gently on my outstretched hand,
Giving me a moment of sheer delight,
To behold a being so pure and gentle.
My heart rejoices and rebounds with warmth,
But by the very warmth is she able to exist
No more in her immaculate whiteness:
She is no longer the white dancing girl;
She has become a lady of compassion.

She has turned into a droplet of water –
The symbol of my tears of sorrow and of joy.

My group's first project was to horse trek some 50 km to a school in Nireguao, near the border with Argentina, to repair a school playground and to interact with the students. To do that, we had to first learn how to handle a horse, to mount and dismount from one, and to secure our equipment and supplies to one. Having had a few horse-riding lessons in my first year of university, interacting with a horse was not an entirely new skill for me. However, in my eagerness to familiarize myself with the horse assigned to me, I forgot a pertinent ground rule: never walk behind a horse! When I did that, the nervy creature gave me a back thrust with one of its hind legs. It left a distinct horse-shoe mark on the back of my right knee. Thank God I withstood the blow and continued the expedition despite the pain.

The horse trek project was a novelty for most of the participants. Led by Kristina, an Operation Raleigh staff member, and assisted by a local Chilean cowboy, Luis, the group travelled eastward, first to Dos Lagunas and then to Coyhaique Alto, covering a distance of about 35 km over two days. The pace was painfully slow, but the beauty of the far-stretching countryside more than compensated for the lack of speed. The interminable path stretched on, up and down the slopes, round corners, down numerous streams and across many make-shift bridges. The landscape was not simply one of undulating slopes with intermittent lines and patches of snow; yonder, by chance would appear a predatory bird up on a solitary tree rendering us its most melodious tune. It was magical, magic of the wildest wilderness.

However, truth be told that the horse trek was not all smooth and flowing without any menace. The vast open terrain was an invitation for the wind to indulge in its playfulness as it stirred up a troupe of dancing sand which turned and tossed around and about us, causing us to transform into different characters: Alex wrapped himself up to look like Lawrence of Arabia; Karen covered her head and turned into a little green-riding-hood; Kristina took on the role of a mysterious Middle Eastern lady, all hidden save her pair of penetrative eyes. We were all at the mercy of the wind, the cold, the sand and the dust of this land. Still, carried by the horses, we ploughed on with perseverance.

From Coyhaique Alto, we turned north to Nireguao, covering some 30 km over two days. In the evening, the horses huddled together for warmth and protection while each of us built our own bivouacs and disappeared into them. On one of the nights, I chose a rather secluded spot for my bivouac for some solitary existence. As I was luxuriating in my enjoyment of the song *Messiah* through my cassette player, two dogs belonging to the farm we were at came to lie on top of my sleeping bag, supposedly for warmth. Not wanting the additional weight on me, I nudged and pushed them away. However, in the wee hours of the morning, they must have returned and finding the solitary camper asleep, nestled round the peripheral of my shelter. I woke several times throughout the night due to the icy cold air, sensing movements all around me. So it was not such a solitary existence after all!

When we arrived at the school in Nireguao, a group of expectant elementary school children were there to welcome us. They must have been told of our coming to repair the school playground. The playground was still usable but some of the wooden apparatuses were in a state of disrepair. Also, for unknown reasons, there were ditches here and there which made the field unsafe for the children to run on. After a few days of trekking on horseback, all of us were ready to put our hands to good use: some filled the ditches, while others looked into replacing some wooden poles and planks for the apparatuses on the playground. We were all game for some manual work.

Our time working on the school playground was punctuated by the appearance of the school children when they came out to play during their breaks. Through our conversation with them, we learned some Spanish words and knew more about the culture of Chile, while the children learned some English words from us. On a particular Friday afternoon, Eric, one of the boys who often came to talk to us, invited me to spend the weekend with him at his uncle's house at El Gato village, some 15 km from Nireguao, where a festival involving horse racing would take place. I was naturally keen to go as it was a once-in-a-lifetime opportunity. However, since I was part of the expedition group, I had to consult the team leader, Kristina. Was I glad she gave me the green light to enjoy myself with Eric over the weekend!

The weekend at El Gato had its familial warmth. I was transported to a three-generational family comprising Eric's grandparents, his uncle and children. For a change, I had a proper bed instead of a sleeping bag to sleep in, and home-cooked food instead of pre-packed ration. But more than the material comfort was the opportunity to have a glimpse into the life of a typical Chilean family in a rural setting. The family house was set amidst a huge plot of land on which they reared chickens and ducks. Although I did not come across any sheep farm at El Gato, the presence of mutton at every main meal with the family convinced me that sheep farming must be rather common in that region. Much later, through research, I found that sheep farming is indeed extensive across the Patagonian grasslands, making the southern regions of both Chile and Argentina a world-famous sheep farming area.

The highlight of the weekend was supposed to be a horse race in El Gato. By mid day that Saturday, the weather had turned sufficiently warm, and many families had come from surrounding villages on their domesticated horses in anticipation of watching some exciting horse races. A number of cowboys, dressed in indigenous wool tunics and sheepskin pants were getting ready for the event which would be conducted on the dual horse tracks. However, as is typical in mountainous regions, the capricious weather changed rather rapidly; the slight drizzle soon turned into rain. After watching the first race, Eric and I decided to head indoors. That was when he showed me his collection of books on the two great World Wars. I was impressed by his desire for general knowledge but unfortunately our conversation could not go deeper, since I was hindered by my limited Spanish and he, his limited English.

The highlight of my time in El Gato, which happened on Sunday, was about food. After a luxurious hot shower in the morning, I was treated to a simple but delicious lunch prepared by Eric's grandmother: a glass of wine served with mutton soup, potatoes, and fried mutton wrapped in breadcrumbs. It was more than a meal; it spoke of her love for the guest of her grandson who had come from the Far East. In the afternoon, at my request, she taught me how to bake Chilean bread, both unleavened and leavened ones. I copied the recipes in my diary lest I should lose them through scraps of paper. Watching her dexterous hands kneading the dough so effortlessly was itself a delight to me.

Upon my return to Nireguao, I rejoined the group and worked on repairing the goalposts of the football field. On another day, some of us started to erect a new fence around the field. For some reason, I began making baseball bats out of pieces of wood and found it really enjoyable. To me, every stroke of the carving knife in rounding the edges of the bats was a stroke of art; the bats when finished and put to use would bring about moments of excitement and exhilaration for the children. In general, they seemed to enjoy the game though not everyone had the opportunity or the confidence to bat. In addition to baseball, I also taught some children simple gymnastic movements on the narrow beam and horizontal bar.

Towards the end of our time at the school, we had a mini celebration with the school teachers and children. On 16th October, Teachers' Day in Chile, the headmaster initiated the celebration by dancing with one of the teachers. Soon, all of us from the horse trek group joined in the dancing, followed by the children. It was a simple and spontaneous way of celebrating Teachers' Day. Then each of us from Operation Raleigh introduced ourselves briefly in Spanish, and this was followed by an English lesson and a few games conducted by us for the children. It was a time of good fun and general chaos. Eager to win every game, the students cheated and then swarmed around Suzanne, the judge, to declare their victory. However, at the end of all the games, 'justice' was meted out and everyone was satisfied as each was rewarded with sweets and more sweets.

The two weeks on horseback and in Nireguao were fleeting. Soon we had to bid farewell to the school teachers and children, as well as Kristina and Alex, and move on to the next project. Ian, a captain in the British army and the leader of our next project, met us at Nireguao to brief us on the project. Essentially, it was a two-week trekking expedition in the mountains. We had the option to conquer either distance or altitude, and the group chose the latter, much to my delight. This meant that we would be spending a number of nights above the snow line, which was an entirely new experience for me.

Sufficient preparation for an alpine climb was important, especially for novices like most of us in the group. Ian showed us his personal kit as he briefed us on the essential packing list. To reduce the weight of our backpacks, we were instructed to leave out unnecessary things which would be transported back to FHQ by the support staff. The entire group was also issued with four North Face dome tents used by the previous Operation Raleigh team in Alaska; three or four members were to share a tent and the parts of a tent were to be distributed among the members for packing. We were also given lessons on assembling and dismantling the tents, as well as setting up the bulky radio set for communication with FHQ.

The day of preparation added to my sense of expectancy and excitement. I was up the next morning at about half past six to finish my packing which included seven days of ration, stainless steel anti-slip crampons for my hiking boots (to walk on hardened snow), ice-axe, harness, two carabiners, a short rope, flysheet for our dome-shaped tent, and a spare heavy battery for the radio set, in addition to my personal clothing. It was the heaviest backpack I had ever carried but the thought of adventure soon put the weight out of my mind. I believe this was also the mindset of many others in the group.

The group finally set off at about 9 a.m. on 21st October 1991, after a brief photo session. We trekked along the bottom of Nireguao valley, crossed undulating fields, and entered the woods; for every hour of trekking, we gave ourselves ten minutes of rest. We also stopped a longer time for lunch. Along the way, we feasted our eyes on some of the most beautiful scenery: snow-capped mountains, green meadows, horses grazing, streams flowing round pebbles and glimmering occasionally in the sunlight. My heart was so enraptured by the beauty of nature all around me that I soon forgot about the heavy burden on my back. Yes, nature enveloped me and I became one with nature!

In the later part of the afternoon, after climbing further slopes, we agreed to look for a suitable campsite near a running stream to spend the night. We found a fairly flat ground and soon went about our routine, according to the daily roster: some to erect the four dome-shaped tents, which were easy to pitch and light to carry; others to collect firewood to start a fire for boiling water and cooking dinner; still others to set up the radio set to report our location to the FHQ. During dinner, Ian our leader reported that we had covered about 17 km that day. It was an impressive record, considering the fact that it was the first day of our trek and we were carrying extremely heavy packs.

On the second day, we decided to keep our campsite as a base camp and make a lightweight attempt at scaling the mountain peak ahead of us. This would also give us an idea if it was possible for us to carry our full packs over the peak the following day. Without the heavy load weighing down on our backs, we moved faster up the slopes, using our ice axes to aid us in our ascent. However, the higher we ascended, the deeper the snow; by the time we reached the top of the tree line, the snow was around four to six feet deep, submerging the tree trunks and revealing only the top branches. Just above the tree line, we stopped for lunch and had one of the most magnificent views on earth: snow-capped mountain range in the distance, and valleys and meandering rivers below. The green, the brown and the white blended so naturally and seamlessly that the entire scene spoke to me of God's masterful hand behind its beauty.

After lunch, the group split into two. One went further ahead to try to locate a lake some four km further north-west, while the other retraced our steps to our base camp to start preparing dinner. I was in the latter group. Initially, the going was easy as we simply followed the footprints left in the snow during our ascent. However, as we descended further, most of the snow had melted and so did our footprints. Thus we had to rely on some markings on tree trunks to ascertain the direction. Finally, with Karen (who remained behind in the base camp to keep the fire going) sounding her whistle, we found our way back to our light blue dome-shaped tents and boiled some water for coffee and tea. Just as the water was boiling, the other group returned. Around the fire we sat with our cups of hot coffee or tea and discussed the plan for the next day: early start to take full advantage of the hardened snow. This meant that my buddy, Andy, and I had to wake at 5 o'clock the next morning to light the fire and boil water for the group. That was our assigned duty according to the roster!

The third day was full of promise. We had breakfast in the breaking hour of dawn and were all packed and ready to move off by 7 a.m. With renewed strength and the snow in its hardened form, we made good progress in our ascent, reaching the previous day's lunch point in two and a half hours despite bearing our full packs, the same amount of time it took us the day before when we went lightweight. Seizing the ample time ahead of us, Ian brought us to a steep snow-clad slope to learn ice-axe braking – executing an emergency brake using an ice axe. First, we were asked to slide down a slope on our bottom while holding an ice axe in front; it was great fun. Then we were taught how to roll over onto our front while sliding and use the ice axe to brake the fall; one at a time we executed this, under the watchful eyes of our project leader, Ian. This important skill gave us the confidence to operate in snow-filled mountains.

After lunch, we plodded on in search of a small lake some 4 km from us. However, after covering that distance and more, the lake was still not within sight. By this time, our packs were weighing heavily down on us as we had to lift our legs continuously from the sunken snow. Ian then suggested we put our packs down and go in separate directions to look for possible sources of water from beneath the snow. We did, but all our efforts were in vain. Finally, we decided to camp on the snow, using and rationing whatever remaining water we had in our water bottles till we found water the next day.

The water crisis turned into a blessing beyond imagination. Upon the white open expanse of immaculate snow, we pitched our tents next to one another in a circular formation, with the entrances facing inward so that we could cook, eat and discuss as a group the proceedings for the next day. That formation would also provide us with some protection against the cold wind. It was then that Laurie, a support staff who brought along a gas stove, dug a hole in the middle of the circle created by the four tents to boil some hot water for us. He was in fact melting the snow! We were amazed by his ingenuity, and overjoyed that despite our apparent lack of water, we could be enjoying a cup of hot drink high up in the mountains.

A greater surprise awaited some of us. While the group was preparing dinner, Ian our project leader had gone further upslope to dig a snow hole for one of the ladies, who must have earlier complained about the lack of space for the four of them in their dome tent. At 6 p.m., when Ian brought Suzanne and Maggie to look at the snow hole, I went along to find out how it looked like. I was stupefied and fascinated at the same time. It was an elongated hole in the slope, just long enough for a sleeping mat and a sleeping bag on top of it, dug with the aid of an ice axe and a mess tin as a shovel. It was simple yet extraordinary to me! I expressed my intention to dig one for myself, and Ian readily agreed.

That was a once-in-a-lifetime experience. It took me one and a half hours to dig my own snow hole. In the process, I got wet, drenched and soaked to the skin. Satisfied with the length of the hole, I went back to the tent to change into dry clothes. Andy, my buddy, had kindly helped to prepare dinner in the meantime; Ian the project leader had also sacrificially exchanged his sleeping bag, which can keep one warm up to minus 15 degree Celsius, with mine which is good up to zero degree Celsius. At 8.30 p.m., under the weak illumination of the moon, Suzanne, Maggie and I made our way to our respective snow holes. Once inside the snow hole, I fell asleep almost immediately. There was nothing much to do save to rejoice in this newfound experience, this most solitary solitude.

I slept so well in the snow hole that I thought I had found a haven of peace and perfect rest - heaven. But I did wake up at about 3 o'clock in the stillness of the morning. I peeped through the entrance of the hole to the world outside and was momentarily intoxicated and mesmerized by the brightness and fullness of the moon. It was so big and near; I could scarce withstand her bold and bright stare. With streamlined eyes, I acknowledged her awesome beauty. She had conquered the darkness looming over this whiteness; she had also inspired me to write creatively under her radiance. I penned my experience of sleeping in a snow hole:

Embrace

She lay motionless, showing no fear nor fright
As I advanced.
I stood before her and surveyed
Her curvature.
No! She had no coyness in her!
Beautiful and white,
Her bareness reflected
Her extreme fairness.
                    I knocked.
I dug into her deepest bosom,
Creating a space for myself
In her warmest embrace.

The next morning, Suzanne, Maggie and I reported a very warm and comfortable night of rest while those who slept in tents complained of the freezing cold throughout the night.

The objective of the fourth day was to conquer the summit of Co Los Huemules, northwest from our campsite, without our backpacks. As we started the day late, the going was difficult as the snow was beginning to melt by the time we started scaling the peak. At one point, the snow was almost up to our thighs and it was strenuous to lift our legs high up as we gained altitude. Nevertheless, the group ploughed on persistently and reached the end of the ridge beyond the summit. From there, we could survey the surrounding valleys and mountains, and look for possible routes of advance for the following week after our resupply at El Gato. Back at our campsite, we discussed the various routes to descend the mountain, and finally chose one that headed in the northeasterly direction.

Contrary to our expectation, it was not an easier way to descend. Not only had we to wade through thigh-deep snow but we also had to contend with the heavily wooded slopes, negotiating round tree trunks and avoiding overhanging branches. By the time we cleared the snow line, we were wet through, and some were battered and bruised by the overhanging branches which slammed into them. With dogged perseverance, we trudged downhill and came to a dry, flat and sunny area. Here, by a stream, we set up camp for the night. Though our physical energy was sapped, our spirits were high. In the evening, after our dinner, Ian who hailed from Scotland, taught us some Scottish songs, one of which was *Flower of Scotland* which we sang with much gusto again and again. That night, long after the rest had gone to bed, I remained by the embers and allowed my thoughts to flow into a poem:

I Write in the Full Moon Shine

I write in the full moon shine
By the fire, before a still tree,
Staring at the flames, dancing
Frivolously, sending sparks into the wind.

Warming socks, boots and all
Who gathered round her in songs,
Of pure Scottish strain, singing
Passionately, deep into the night.

Decorated by stars hanging high
Up in the sky, the full moon shines,
Outlining the size and shape
Of all the surrounding mountain peaks.

Beckoning us in our daily trek,
Embracing us in our nightly rest.

The fifth day was rather uneventful compared to the first four days. We were traversing mostly on low grounds splattered with pockets of snow. According to plan, we reached a lake 4 km away in good time. After a lunch stop, we continued trekking towards El Gato, where some expected to satisfy their cravings for chocolate and biscuits at a provision store in the village. We dragged our feet over 6 km or more of a track strewn with rocks and stones, brushing aside the physical tiredness we felt within and the discomfort caused by the uneven surfaces on which we walked. Soon, we arrived at El Gato. Under the guidance of the carabineros (local police), we were directed to spend the night in the large compound of a local family, that belonging to Eric's grandparents. For me, it was El Gato revisited. In the evening, after dinner and around the fire, our conversation drifted to the topic of education. We aired our opinions on the values of higher education and was there a keen debate!

Bright sunshine greeted us the next morning. As agreed previously, we had a late breakfast at 8.30 a.m. so that we could lie in our sleeping bags longer than usual. Then, half the group set off on a recce for possible rock climbing and camping sites while the rest of us simply attended to our personal tasks such as washing clothes and writing letters to family and friends. For me, I also used the opportunity to update my diary entries, and spent some time interacting with Eric and his grandparents. It was like a home-coming for me. In the late afternoon, the resupply vehicle came with our ration for the next six days. And more importantly, it delivered our incoming mail and collected our outgoing mail. This service kept us in contact with the world beyond the Patagonian mountains.

Having experienced so much in the first week of trekking, the second week was more predictable and manageable. We spent two days rock climbing and abseiling from rock faces, and another two traversing up and down Mount Negro. The highlight of the second week for me was our attempt to dig a snow hole big enough to house all the twelve of us. The event was recorded in my diary as follows:

As we neared the proud snowy peak,
Ian the project leader began to dig:
Two snow holes to house twelve persons –
For many of us, it was a new lesson.
In addition, Brenda made a loo with a view –
A majestic seat – for us the select few.
Three hours passed but the holes were not complete,
Digging snow holes never proved an easy feat.
Laurie sensibly left to cook tomato fusilli for dinner,
While Scottish Ian wandered off to peaks far higher.
Before dark, one snow hole was ready
To fit nine venturers and mad Maggie,

While Ian and Laurie gallantly volunteered
To spend the night in a smaller shelter.
Lastly, a brew to warm our bodies –
'Tis a tiring day – good night, buddies!

By the end of the two weeks, I had learned some survival skills regarding camping and mountain climbing above the snow line. Incidentally, I also acquired some musicality to appreciate and sing some Scottish songs. In a letter that Joan wrote to me from Loughborough in early October 1991, which I received in Nireguao on 10th October 1991, she assured me that her 'love and prayers [will] continue to surround [me]'. Indeed, in the past five weeks in Chile, I had felt His gentle hands upon me, protecting and sustaining me.

CHAPTER 14

Of Hanging Glaciers and Marine Life in Chile (Part 2)

The sea is his, for he made it, and his hands formed the dry land.
Psalm 95:5

Upon our return from El Gato to FHQ, we found out that our group would be split into two smaller groups, each merged with a smaller group from another big group. The purpose of this reorganization was to enable us to get to know more participants. However, I would keep my buddy Andy for the remaining two projects. This was comforting as we had gotten used to each other after sharing a tent for a month, though it also meant that I had to put up with his frequent farting for another month!

At this mid-point of our time in Chile, we were given four days of rest and assigned duties. Apart from attending to our personal tasks such as washing our clothes and replenishing some essentials from the local stores, we were assigned some work at a local orphanage near Coyhaique and in FHQ itself. At the orphanage, we repaired some tables and benches, removing broken planks and replacing them with new ones, painted a mural on the outer wall of the main building, and organized a party for the children; in FHQ, we had to clean and maintain the entire compound including the shower cubicles, the kitchen, the dining area, the store rooms, and the field on which we pitched our tents.

After a few days of hiatus at FHQ, we were ready to set off for our third project at Queulat National Park on 7th November 1991. The objective of the project was to build a path in the national park so as to provide visitors with easy access to some vantage points. To do that, we needed to learn how to use a chain saw as we would be cutting some thick tree trunks and logs. When Richard, our project leader, finally emerged from his meeting with CONAF (National Forest Corporation) staff at about 3 p.m., we loaded up onto the Operation Raleigh vehicle and travelled more than 210km northward to Queulat National Park. The journey took us four and a half hours over gravel tracks. By the time we arrived, we had just enough time to set up our tents and eat our dinner before night fell.

The next morning, Richard gave us a detailed briefing and orientation of the park which consists of virgin evergreen forests. He then brought us some distance up to look at the path completed thus far by the previous two groups. It was impressive. We could see the hard work they put in to clear the dense vegetation in order to lay the path. Subsequently, we were given instructions for the extension of the path. The work would involve clearing a path through the thick undergrowth and using logs to pave the trail so that the soil would not erode. After lunch back at the base camp, we set off to work immediately. It was hard work but we were prepared to undertake the task.

Queulat National Park is famous for its hanging glaciers, one of which is literally hanging above a cliff. Most visitors to the park come for this spectacular view. However, when it rains (and it rains rather frequently in the park), the glacier would be obscured by the clouds or rain. Thus, on the fourth day, when the sun came out in its full radiance, our group decided to take a walk towards the glacier to have a closer view of its splendor. With a day pack containing food behind each of our back, we trekked about 3.3 km along the side of the river through rapids and dense forest to the best viewpoint in the park overlooking the glacier hanging above a cliff. From the glacier, the constantly melting water creates two towering waterfalls, and ice is continuously falling and crashing from the top of the glacier to the bottom of the moraine, creating a rumbling noise that echoes in the valley. It was an awe-inspiring scene. We lingered for some time to soak in the grandeur, and some of us captured it on our sketchpads.

Apart from the routine work of extending the path, which occupied us from 9a.m. to 5 p.m. each day, there was ample time for us to indulge in our personal pursuits. In the few days before we departed for Queulat National Park, encouraged by one of my group members, I bought a harmonica in one of the stores in Coyhaique. At someone else's recommendation, I also procured a photocopied anthology of poems by Pablo Neruda, the most famous Chilean poet who won the Nobel Prize for Literature in 1971. These I brought with me to the project site so that in my solitary moments, I might teach myself to play the harmonica and read the poems. In addition, I also tried to learn Spanish from my phrase book since my new group now consisted of Mariela, a participant from Chile, who could help me with the language.

One morning, while trying to cut some logs, a few of us found the chain saw malfunctioning. One of the parts was kaput and thus we decided to head to the nearest village, Puyuhuapi, for its replacement. Located some 21 km north of the park, Puyuhuapi is a charming village nestled at the head of the fjord. The calm and pristine blue water gave this small village a serenity all its own. We walked into a provision store and were amazed by the abundance of food supply displayed on the shelves behind the counter: canned food, cereal, Milo drink, biscuits, chocolate bars and a whole lot more. Three young Chilean ladies were at our service: one handed us the goods we wanted, another wrote a receipt, and the last collected the amount in cash from us. It was a strict division of labour. I left the shop wandering if it was due to a lack of jobs that they were thus employed and deployed in the store.

Back at the national park, the progress on the path was moving according to expectation. According to the original plan, Richard proposed a five-day trek to a particular gorge in the park for half the group, while the other half could continue to work on the path. The decision to go on the trek or to remain behind to work on the path was left entirely to us. Based on the physical conditions of our bodies, and our own preference for more or less climbing and scrambling, we were first to make a personal decision and then collectively a group decision. Eager to see more of nature in its purest and wildest form, I made up my mind to put my body through the rigorous trek.

The trekking group consisted of seven: Richard, four male and two female participants. The weather was cool and pleasant on the day we set off. With our backpacks laden with essentials and ration for five days, we set off in high spirits. As we trekked on scree, rocks and boulders, often next to a stream, we could see a layer of mist rising in the distance, as though guiding us further and deeper into the virgin forests. Here and there, there were huge fallen tree trunks across the gently flowing streams, aiding and at times obstructing our passage. We also crossed rope bridges secured over gushing rivers, jumped from one boulder to another and scrambled up mossy rock faces. At times, from a vantage point, we could see the mighty water rushing down the river with such horsepower as to drown anybody attempting to cross it. Through it all, I felt the vastness of nature enveloping us; we were like seven tiny ants making our way slowly and painfully into the deep interior. Before last light, we had found a suitable campsite where we set up shelters and replenished our energy with food.

The second day was wet and dampening in spirit. It rained, and continued to pour the entire day. Our advance into the interior was slowed down as we had to traverse across wet and slippery terrain. We did not talk much, as our voices were drowned by the sound of the splattering rain on the leaves and branches. To add to my misery, my whole body was becoming soaking wet as the windbreaker and pants I had on me were not waterproof, and my damp socks were making my boots heavier as the hours went by. The experience reminded me of my time in the jungle of Brunei, except that it was much colder here in the southern part of Chile. At long last, we reached the top of the gorge, but the demoralizing rain had erased any jubilation that we felt within.

Within the group, there were differing opinions about exploring further beyond the gorge. We did advance initially, but later decided to retreat. When last light was about to dawn on us at 9 p.m., we set up camp, cooked dinner, changed into dry clothes and withdrew into our sleeping bags. For many of us, perhaps all, it was a cold, wet and sleepless night. I was shivering in my bag which progressively became damp; my head was aching as a result of the physical exertion and the biting cold. I could not remember what went through my mind in those lonesome hours of darkness and dampness, for I did not record any notes in my diary, but I was sure I longed for the sun to rise to warm my body.

In the late morning on the third day, after breakfast, Andy, the trek leader of the day, called for a meeting. Both of us had earlier talked about returning to base camp a day earlier because of the unfavorable weather condition, and the weakening state of our body. A brief discussion ensued and each individual expressed their opinion and preference – to spend the third day exploring or to begin to head back. It was a split decision: four against three were in favor of returning a day earlier, and I was one of the four. Having had little sleep the night before, and having changed back into my wet clothing (so as to keep the dry set for the night), I was not keen to explore further and deeper into the interior of this virgin forest.

A democratic decision was made to begin our return journey. For the four of us who voted to go back, it was a relief beyond words; for the other three who were intent to explore further, it was a surrender of the will to submit to the decision of the majority. Our intention was to reach the first night's campsite at the end of the day. In the persistent rain, we carried our feet over the terrain which we trampled the day before. I was still suffering from the effects of chill; however, the decision to turn back had somehow lifted my spirit so much so that I began to think of roti prata[38] and other Singaporean food, and my parents in Singapore. Such longing for home seldom struck me in my years of wandering in different parts of the world.

The third night, to shield ourselves from the wind, my buddy Andy and I chose to sleep on a huge slab of rock in a cavern. Little did we realize that the temperature in a cavern could be colder than the ground surface as rocks tend to retain the heat or the cold for a longer period of time compared to soil. Throughout the night, I was shivering in my damp sleeping bag, made worse by the cold emanating from the rock surface on which I lay. In the wee hours of the morning, I moved my sleeping bag closer to my buddy's to share his body warmth. In the morning, for breakfast, I emptied five sachets of sugar and four sachets of milk powder into my porridge to give myself more instant energy and nutrients for the final day of trekking.

The final day of trekking was one of mind over the body. Physically, we were tired; mentally, we were persevering with grit. Descending the mountains with strained muscles in our legs could be dangerous; we trod with care lest we should tumble and fall. As our speed slowed, I was able to take time to appreciate the flowers that grew in the wild; I also once again marveled at the gigantic proportion of nature in terms of the size of the boulders and the height of the trees. They loomed over

---

[38] Roti prata is an Indian-influenced flatbread dish found in several countries in Southeast Asia, including Brunei, Indonesia, Malaysia and Singapore

us, like Cyclops over tiny men of valour. O, how nature dwarfed us and made us so insignificantly small!

By mid-day, we had already descended to the lower reaches of the national park. The ground temperature was obviously warmer and the sun was welcoming our return to low land. While we were having lunch, one of the group members asked everyone what they thought of returning a day earlier. It seemed a superfluous question to me: we had already made the descent from the gorge and it would be pointless to go back on our decision at this juncture. Any discussion on that question would at best be an intellectual discourse of no practical consequence or value. The question hung in the air, as we trudged our feet along the river back to our base camp. We made it back by 8 p.m. and were glad to join the other six who remained behind, sharing stories of the trek with them.

The question about our decision to turn back a day earlier continued to hang in the air for a few more weeks. It was not till the end of the entire expedition when all of us had returned to London that I was sure that the decision to turn back was a sound and necessary one. In a store selling outdoor equipment near Shepherd's Bush London Underground station, I bought a book *Mountaincraft and Leadership* written by Eric Langmuir. In one of the chapters, I read about the symptoms of hypothermia, and immediately realized that I was experiencing the onset of hypothermia while trekking in the mountains of Queulat National Park: "feeling cold and tired with perhaps some numbness of the hands and feet and intermittent bouts of shivering."[39] As I looked back at the episode, I thanked God for sustaining me.

---

[39] Quoted from *Mountaincraft and Leadership* by Eric Langmuir, page 195.

Arriving back at base camp a day earlier also meant that we had an extra day of work on the path. Next morning, with a sense of purpose, we picked up our equipment and continued to work on the path till 4 p.m., despite our lethargy and sore muscles. It was our final contribution to this park before we moved on to our next project at Puerto Raul Marin Balmaceda the following day. That evening, the resupply vehicle came, and with it, three letters for me. Once again, through the letters, I was momentarily lured into the worlds of my family and friends in different countries such as England, Tunisia and Singapore.

On 20th November 1991, our group loaded our backpacks unto the back of an Operation Raleigh vehicle and travelled some 66 km north to La Junta. It was a bumpy ride on gravel tracks and the jolting motion soon caused me to fall asleep. By the time I woke up, we had arrived at the launching point of the next leg of our journey, a short distance outside the village of La Junta. A motor boat was waiting for us.[40] We loaded our baggage and were soon making our way down River Palena to Port Raul Marin Balmaceda, located at the mouth of the river, facing the South Pacific Ocean, at latitude 43.8 degree South. This is almost the same latitude as Christchurch, a city in the South Island of New Zealand.

Journeying down the river from La Junta to Marin Balmaceda was like going back to the earliest of times. The vegetation on both sides of the river was thick and virgin. Tall, slender, and gigantic trees towered over us

---

[40]   Back in 1991, the only way to get to Marin Balmaceda from La Junta was by boat. A 72.9 km road now links La Junta to Marin Balmaceda, and the journey takes around 2 hours 15 minutes.

and reigned supreme in this remote part of the earth. Apart from us, no other human souls were in sight as we sailed down the serpentine river. The distant and indomitable mountains stood large and cold, showing disinterest in our coming. The wind, on the other hand, blew mightily over us, and the waves knocked against out boat as though resenting our approach and jealously guarding the land. Still, Juan, the boatman ploughed on, braving all hostile elements opposing our efforts to reach our destination.

As far as I remember, there was no Operation Raleigh staff leading us on this project. Instead, a local by the name of Rachelle, possibly a wealthy Chilean who owned a few local properties, was the coordinator of this project. In these final two weeks, we were to repair some paths in Marin Balmaceda and to enjoy the stunning and unspoiled nature around us, especially marine life. En route to our destination, we stopped at Rachelle's resort. It was heart-warming to be welcomed into the cozy and warm resort with freshly baked buns and steaming hot tea waiting for us. Instantly, we associated Marin Balmaceda with the special hospitality found in rural remote villages, which, like its scenery, had no equal in bigger towns and cities.

The weather in the southern part of Chile is known to be cool and wet throughout the year. On the second and third day of our time at Marin Balmaceda, it rained so heavily that we were unable to get out to do any work, or to saunter on the endless white beaches and climb the nearby sandy dunes. Naturally, I seized the opportunity to read, write and learn Spanish. I perused the books I brought with me and Pablo Neruda's anthology of poems; I wrote many letters to family and friends, and a poem for K whom I had not seen (since our meeting in New York) or heard from for almost three years:

Tonight I Can Write

Tonight I can write,
Write about the serenity of Marin Balmaceda –
Her beauty, stillness, and calm.
Write about the soft tender sand,
And the gentle rippling waters.

Write about the mysterious mountains
Hiding behind the grey overcast skies.
Write about the broken sea-shells
Lying forlorn on the sea-shores.

Tonight I will write,
Write in remembrance of that feeling of love,
Of affection, mutual and strong.
Write about your sweet dimpled smile,
And your long flowing soft hair.
Write about your coy playful manner,
Insisting on my vows of love for you.
Write about those brief happy moments,
And the long inevitable silence.

Tonight I shall ask;
Ask God to touch you.

Tonight I will sing
A lovely birthday song.

For you.
Tonight.

The community work we were tasked to do involved laying a path beside a waterfall, depth survey, and general maintenance of a gym. Compared to the work completed in Queulat National Park, the demands at Marin Balmaceda seemed very manageable. We laboured for a few days and, weather permitting, played volleyball on the beach in the evening. It was like a holiday camp: we worked, we played, and we were looking forward to a two-day outing by boat to fish in a nearby lake. However, we were at the dictates of the capricious weather and could only launch out on a fair day with little wind and no rain.

The fair day finally arrived on 29th November 1991. After a day of holdup by the adverse weather conditions, we finally set off from Marin Balmeceda to Lake Trebol. Packed into two inflatable motorized boats, each steered by a local boatman, we navigated northward in the South Pacific Ocean for some time. At that time, the ocean was a picture of calm waters; the sun had not risen above the blanket of clouds; the surrounding mountains, shrouded in layers of hanging mist, looked mystical and beyond reach. We were lulled into a false sense of calmness and tranquility.

The deception was unraveled once we entered the mouth of River Tictoc. Navigating upstream, our boats battled against the rough waters. The current swelled and swung us up, and let us down, and swung us up again. At some points, the force of the current that pushed against our boats was so great that we were lifted five to ten metres above the water level, with our boats suspended in mid air, almost perpendicular to the water below. Then, pulled by gravity, our boats would fall through the air and land on the rough waters again with a 'bang'. This constant motion of being tossed up and down went on for some time; we gripped the ropes on the sides of the boats for fear of being thrown out of the vessels into the turbulent waters.

All of a sudden, it dawned on me that a precious part of me might have already been jettisoned. Putting my hand into my pocket, I confirmed my suspicion that my waterproof camera had been tossed to the waves. It was not secured to my windbreaker and there was no zip to lock it in the pocket. This unexpected loss caused me momentarily to question the goodness of God: 'Why did this happen to me?' Just as swiftly, another voice within me reminded me of a Bible verse I had memorized since my second year of university: 'Give thanks in all circumstances, for this is God's will for you in Christ Jesus.' (1 Thessalonians 5:18). Upon this reminder, I resolved to give thanks to God. I reasoned within myself: The camera that I lost can be replaced easily, but I should not lose my joy in the Lord, which is priceless.

The fast flowing waters soon gave way to a state of tranquility as we neared Lake Trebol. The lake was a picture of perfect peace. All around, mountains surrounded the lake, as though embracing it. In the still blue water, the lake mirrored the sky and the low lying green hills. Our boatman informed us that in summer months, rich American tourists paid fat dollars to come to this lake for fishing. We went in search of their campsites, and from a distance, spotted patches of blue (color of a tent) amongst the green vegetation. Upon landing on a small strip of beach, we also found a kitchen cabinet with food, some equipment, a rowing boat, and some fuel for outboard motors. In addition, there was a 'civilized' toilet seat – a most unthinkable luxury for a back-to-nature fishing trip!

Given the remoteness of this lake, we decided that our abode for the night should be made of more basic and natural materials. Seizing the availability of bamboo near our campsite, we used bamboo strips and ponchos to erect shelters for ourselves, modeled after the dome-shaped tents that we used on our alpine trek. My buddy Andy even used bamboo strips and leaves to build fencing around our shelter to shield us from the wind. How ingenious! It reminded me of my scouting days in secondary school when bamboo was used extensively to build structures and to cook food with.

Having set up our tents, it was time to relax, unwind or go fishing. Half the group left with the boatman to go fishing, while the rest of us enjoyed a time of siesta in the tranquility of the lake. To keep up my relationship with God and my need for intellectual stimulation, I spent some time reading my small Bible and *Death of a Guru*, a book I bought in New Delhi. I had been reading the book for some weeks now and wanted to finish reading it before the end of the expedition. When the fishing group came back with their catch, I helped to gut the fish: seven rainbow trout and one salmon. That night, gathered around an open fire, we had grilled and steamed fish for supper. It was delicious.

The weather seemed to alternate between sunshine and rain. The next day, it rained for the greater part of the day. So we remained mostly under our shelters. The day after, when the weather turned fair, we packed and headed back to Rachelle's barn. Going downstream was much easier; we were aided by the current which gave our boats a shove from behind. Still, the boatmen had to be alert to steer the vessels away from shallow waters beside sandy banks. Along the way, we were pleasantly surprised to come across some seals and seagulls sunbathing serenely side by side; they seemed to have a tacit understanding that nature belongs to all species, and all species are part of nature. It was a pity I no longer had my camera with me to capture that scene of peaceful co-existence.

There was more to marine life in this region than just fish, seals and seagulls. On our second last day in Marin Balmaceda, on the way to visit Rachelle's big house at Anihue fronting the South Pacific Ocean, our boatman brought us to visually feast on a colony of sea-lions. A great multitude of them were sprawling on some rock outcrops next to the river. A fascinating sight: big, heavy, authoritative ones; small, timid, adorable ones. Most were lying flat sunbathing on the rocks while others lifted their heads up into the air, as though aware of and protesting against our encroachment upon their privacy. Interspersed among the sea-lions were birds of various sizes, colors and breeds. The most eye-catching of them all were the pelicans; with their long colorful beaks, they easily stood out among the other species. We were enthralled by their stately posture, their heads held high up by the long curvature of their necks, when all of a sudden they flapped their wings, and flew in a straight line over the waters, delighting our eyes for a few moments till we saw them no more in the far horizon.

Rachelle's house at Anihue is really a dream house. Sited next to a stretch of pristine beach, it commands an excellent view of the South Pacific Ocean and the nearby mountains. After a quick lunch, we went to frolic in the cool waters of the ocean, and some found a huge rock outcrop from which they literally dived into the ocean. The waters glittered and sparkled in the warm sunshine, as though celebrating with us the end of our ten-week long expedition in Chile. To top it all, a few local divers diving for clams in the nearby waters came to give us a big bag of clams. In the evening, by a big fire on the beach, we had our most memorable dinner in Marin Balmaceda consisting of pasta, clams, freshly-baked bread rolls and beer. It was a fitting end to our time at this project site.

To bid farewell to the breathtaking nature around me, I tarried on the beach long after the last embers had died off. I slept, in my sleeping bag, on the beach. I wanted to commune with nature, and that experience and intimacy with the waves enabled me to pen my feelings of bliss in a poem the following morning:

Bliss

All nature is bliss and flows and pours:
I wake to a new morn,
Conscious of her knocking on my door,
Ever so persistently,
But gently.

I look out and behold the waves
Rushing to greet me,
Reaching out to lick me,
To lure me deeper
Into her bosom.

The journey back to FHQ in Coyhaique was eventful. First, we were given a treat, a chance to dip ourselves in a hot spring along the way; then, the engine of the boat which was supposed to take us from Marin Balmaceda to La Junta broke down seven km short of our destination. As a result, we had to trek the remaining distance with our backpacks to La Junta, where we would be picked up by two Operation Raleigh wagons. With this unforeseen delay, we were not able to make it back to FHQ that evening but had to spend the night at the forestry hut in Queulat National Park. The consolation was that I received two letters that evening. One was from an Australian couple I met in Kibbutz Nirim in Israel more than four years ago; the other was from my sister studying in Birmingham in the United Kingdom. She informed me that she had bought me a return air ticket from London to Madrid. We would be travelling in Spain for two weeks after my expedition in Chile.

The eleven weeks I spent in Chile had truly been enriching. I enjoyed nature in its rawest form and learned some essential outdoor survival skills, which proved useful the following year when I brought a group of Outdoor Activities Club (ODAC) students to climb Mount Mulu in Sarawak. However, the long period of time away from church had also brought home the point that fellowship with like-minded believers is very important for one's spiritual growth. Throughout the time I spent in Chile, I was practicing a very private faith, worshipping God quietly by myself. There was no encouragement from a fellow believer, save the occasional letters I received from Christian friends from England, Tunisia, India and Singapore.

I resolved to give priority to Christian fellowship upon returning to Singapore and beginning my career as a teacher in my alma mater.

EPILOGUE

Using available time in between teaching semesters to write, I finally completed the last chapter of this book on 23 June 2021.

Writing this book has been an epic journey. Poring over my travel diaries, old photographs and slides, and letters from many friends, I re-lived those precious moments which happened more than thirty years ago, and experienced the extremes of feelings all over again. In particular, writing about Chapter 9 was emotionally draining. There was so much joy as well as pain as I read and re-read the letters I received from K, and some of the ones I sent her. The completion of the chapter produced a declarative effect on me, affirming God's guidance in my relationship with K and my ultimate submission to His higher calling to be equally yoked.

When I first started writing in May 2020, my focus had been on producing an accurate record of the places I visited and the people I encountered. As I progressed from one chapter to another, especially when I was writing about my rough journey in East Africa, it dawned on me that I was recording more than a physical journey through time and space; it was also a testament of my spiritual growth. As much as I prided myself as a man alone not feeling the loneliness of this world, I could not deny the fact that God had been my constant though invisible companion. Repeatedly, God met me at my points of need, be they physical, emotional or spiritual, and often surprised me with His goodness beyond my imagination. Indeed, He was there to walk with me and talk with me on every journey.

As I neared the completion of writing this book, it also occurred to me that though the different chapters focused on different countries, there is a unifying factor that pulls all the chapters together. That factor, or glue, is Loughborough. More specifically, it is about the people in Loughborough that I had grown to love and whose fellowship I cherished. In particular, I wish to mention three lovely couples: Bill and Joan Robertson, Patrick and Helen Crowhurst, and Guy and Rosemary Bookless. After each overseas journey, I would return to Loughborough and drop by at their residences. Even after my expedition in Chile in December 1991, before I flew back to Singapore, I made it a point to travel north from London to Loughborough to visit them.

Long after I left Loughborough, I still corresponded with the three couples.

On 29th March 2014, Bill went home to be with the Lord at a ripe old age of 89. My fond memories of his broad smile and open arms stirred me to write a eulogy for him, a copy of which was sent to Joan and her children:

Your Broad Smile and Open Arms – in memory of Bill Robertson

Bill, we remember your broad smile and open arms.
You radiated with joy and embraced us
Even before we were within huggable distance
At your home in 9 Storer Road, or
At the entrance of Elim Church on Ashby Road.

Your broad smile brightened the day
For one and all whom you greeted;
Your open arms warmeth the heart
Of each and every lonely soul.

Being the very person God made you,
You made our day the way He intended it:
Bringing us cheer and blessed assurance
That we were loved and dearly loved.

Through your love, and dearest Joan's,
We felt our Father's affirming love
Despite our wayward and sinful ways:
The Father's love for His prodigal sons.

Long were those memorable days in Lougborough,
Sweet were those days of fellowship;
The decades in between had not the power
To erase the image of Christ we saw in you.

Then, you received us with your open arms;
Now, let the open arms of our heavenly Father

Embrace you in His deepest bosom
As He speaks gently into your ears:

"Welcome Home, my son!"

In June 2017, I had the good fortune of accompanying my wife on a working trip to London and took the opportunity to visit Joan who had by then been moved to Newcastle-upon-Tyne to be near her eldest daughter, Lynda and son-in-law, David. My wife and I spent a quiet afternoon with Joan, looking at old photographs and reminiscing the good old days in Loughborough. In late January 2021, I heard news of Joan's passage to heaven. She had lived a full life of 91 years, sharing God's love with many overseas students in Loughborough. Upon hearing the news, I shed a few tears, and my tears galvanized my emotions to write a eulogy for Joan, a copy of which was sent to Lynda and David:

> **_Touched by an Angel on Earth_** – in memory of Joan Robertson
>
> Joan, we remember your infectious smile,
> Radiating from your face
> At the entrance of 9 Storer Road,
> Greeting us as we walked into
> The firm embracing arms of Bill, your husband.
>
> Joan, we remember your hospitality,
> Inviting us to a meal
> Of roast beef and Yorkshire pudding,
> Giving us a sense of home
> Away from our homes in Singapore.

Joan, we remember your zest for life,
Sketching still life and landscape
With pencils or water colour,
Filling your creations with pastel hues
That added colours to your rooms.

But most of all, we experienced God's love,
Manifesting itself through you
In simple words and actions,
Filling us with inward joy --
Touched by an angel on earth!

Your departure from here is a loss to us;
Your arrival in heaven is a gain to Him.

My life has truly been touched by the warm and wise people God put across my path in Loughborough and in many other parts of the world. In similar fashion, it is my desire to be a blessing to others when God causes my path to cross theirs. As I draw this book to an end, I think it is fitting for me to share the verses of a song I sang in my secondary school days during the weekly school assembly:

If I can help somebody as I pass along,
If I can cheer somebody with a word or a song,
If I can show somebody he is travelling wrong,
Then my living shall not be in vain!

Then my living shall not be in vain,
Then my living shall not be in vain!
If I can help somebody as I pass along,
Then my living shall not be in vain!

24 June 2021